the
call of a
lifetime

the call of a lifetime

is the ministry God's plan for your life?

keith drury

wesleyan
publishing
house

Indianapolis, Indiana

© 2003 by The Wesleyan Church
Published by Wesleyan Publishing House
Indianapolis, Indiana 46250
Printed in the United States of America
ISBN 0-89827-262-9

To my sons—
David Drury and John Drury

table of contents

preface

the title of this book is *The Call of a Lifetime*, because the ministry is one of the greatest things that you can do with your life. So what makes the ministry such a high calling? Ministry is a high calling because ministers lead and serve the church, and the church is the primary tool that God uses to accomplish His will on earth. Jesus Christ established the church and is its cornerstone. God has built the church through the apostles and other leaders over the last 2000 years. And Jesus promised that the very gates of Hell will not prevail against His church. While the church has often been stained and suffers many weaknesses—after all, it is made up of people like you and me—it is still God's primary plan for bringing His kingdom to earth. A call to the ministry is a call to work full-time with the church. The ministry is thus a high calling.

The ministry is a high calling also because it deals with eternal matters: the Word of God and the souls of men and women. When all the cool video games have passed away and there are no more haircuts to be given, meals to eat, or houses to live in—in short, when earth has passed away—the Word of God and the souls of people will continue, through all eternity. A minister spends his or her whole life dealing with these things of eternal value: it is a high calling.

That doesn't mean that other professions do not have great value—they do. And we can appreciate all of them without diminishing the value of Christian ministry. If God calls you to the ministry you can be sure that you have received a high calling. It is a worthwhile way to invest your life and come to a happy and fulfilled end.

This book is for men and women who are pondering a call to the ministry. While it will be of value for people of any age, it is especially designed for younger people. It is not written about you, but to you, almost as if it were a series of letters or E-mails you'd received from a friend. The book answers basic questions about the ministry, like the ones found at the beginning of each chapter. This book is designed to be read over time, not in a single sitting, so some of the material is repeated here and there as a way of helping you remember.

As you read, it may be helpful for you to see where I'm coming from as the author. Nobody writes in a vacuum; we all have personal biases. The following descriptions of this book may help you understand the ministerial ethos from which I write, and thus you may be able to counterbalance any of my prejudices or errors as you read.

1 this book espouses a high view of the ministry

You will find here a book that does not depreciate the ministry in order to pump up the importance of other vocations. I believe that the ministry is a high and holy calling and that the calling is as old as the Bible itself. I think professional ministry is a wonderful way to spend your life and that you'll get great fulfillment from a life so spent. I believe all Christians are called to minister to others, but some are specifically set apart as apostles, prophets, evangelists, and pastors and teachers. God calls these people to be equipping ministers, and they are His gift to the church (see Eph. 4). I think everybody ought to *want* to be called to the ministry because it is a wonderful way to invest one's life. Yet I believe that not everybody is called. The ministry is limited to those who are called by God and confirmed by the church. If this book fails to raise your view of the ministry, it has failed in one of its primary objectives.

this book is about ordained ministry

Every Christian, of course, is called to minister—to serve others. But some are called by God into lifelong ministry. These are the people the church sets apart, or *ordains*. But there is also a group in between laypeople and ordained ministers: people in full-time religious work who are not ordained. They might be music directors, youth workers, parachurch ministry staffers, camp directors, worship leaders, Christian school teachers, church secretaries, business managers, or any number of others who work full-time doing religious work but are not ordained. There are two major differences between ordained and nonordained church workers: (1) Ordained ministers perform sacred acts which only they are authorized to do, things like presiding at Holy Communion, performing weddings, and preaching regularly. And (2) ordained people are set apart for lifelong service. For them, ministry isn't a temporary job. Sometimes people head into the ministry without knowing this distinction and begin preparing for ordination when they really ought to go into nonordained church work. Both can be full-time jobs in the church, and working as a lay staff person or lay missionary is a good thing to do. This book however, is not written for people who want to work for five years as a lay staffer at a Christian camp and then do something else. It is for people who feel called to lifelong ordained ministry.

this book advocates a clear call to the ministry

The ministry is a wonderful way to invest one's life, but the only people who should enter it are those clearly called by God. There is no test you can take to find out if you should be a minister. There are tests that will tell you if your temperament exhibits some of the personality traits that are important for ministry, or if you have the aptitudes most ministers posses. But these are just evidences to consider; they are not a call from God. God calls men and women to equip, lead, and serve His people. He's done that for thousands of years, and He still does. Your call may come in one of several ways—dramatically or quietly, instantly or gradually—but there is no single indicator that will give you absolute certainty that God has called you to the ministry. You may have only an inkling of this call today, but be assured that if God is calling you to the ministry, He will eventually make your calling sure. <u>If you never feel sure, don't enter the ministry.</u>

4 this book assumes a high view of the church

As important as the personal call is, it is not complete until the church confirms it. Your life in ministry is not between you and God. It is a three-way deal between you, God, and the church. God calls a minister to work with His church, the body of Christ on earth. <u>There are scores of fun and exciting things a person might do in life, but nothing is as exciting and *important* as serving the church.</u> The local church is God's plan to reach the world and make disciples of all nations. There are other tools that He uses, but the church is His *primary* tool. There are other things you can do with your life as an ordained minister (for example, teach other ministers, as I do) but none of them is as important or long lasting as ministering in a local church to the same congregation week after week. You may feel more famous if you travel around and speak at conventions, but that would be a second-place position compared to the pastors, youth pastors, and staff pastors in local churches, who really make the greatest impact on the world. This book will encourage you to think about local church ministry as the best way to do God's work on earth.

5 in this book you will see a lofty view of ordination

You should know that there are some churches who won't agree with the high view of ordination presented in this book. Some churches dismiss the ministry as nothing more than paid laity. There are even a few independent churches that will ordain high school students, then send them to college to prepare for the ministry to which they are already ordained. Occasionally, a church will ordain people just so they can get the break on their taxes. There are a few churches who cast the pearls of ordination before swine, yet most denominations hold a much higher view of ordination, one more in line with the viewpoint of this book. I believe ordination is a sacred vow that should not be taken without serious thought, at least as much thought as should be given to entering marriage. Ordination is not a temporary driver's permit. It is a lifelong commission from the church to be a prophet and priest. Don't get ordained just to try ministry for a few years and see if you like it. If you have that attitude, get a job in the church that doesn't require ordination. Ordination is for people who plan to be lifelong ministers. Something mystical and spiritual actually happens in your ordination service. It is more than an official act, like pledging allegiance to the flag or being inducted into the military. Most denominations expect actual power to come into the person at ordination. They even have a special prayer designed to provide this experience. Your ordination service will be a powerful event where the church will set you apart for ministry. At that moment, God will come and do something in your soul—if you let Him.

this book is written to both men and women

There is a whole chapter in this book for women who are called to the ministry, but it is important for you to know that the writer of this book believes that God calls both men and women into the ministry. And when God calls people, they must obey. The Roman Catholic, Orthodox, and some Protestant denominations do not permit women to be ordained ministers. I think they are wrong and that they will eventually realize it. But until they do, if you are a woman whom God has called, you may have to leave the denomination of your youth in order to find a church who will confirm your call. That may not be fair or nice, yet it is the truth. So when God calls, what are you to do? You must answer His call.

While this book may present a higher view of the ministry, the church, ordination, and the call than you are familiar with, it is not just the personal view of this author, however. It represents the historic position of most denominations. Check your own denomination's view on these matters to see if it differs from this book. You can do that by reading your denomination's ministerial preparation web site or manuals.

acknowledgements

this book is not the product of one person. I am deeply indebted to many people who have helped me develop my thinking and hone the manuscript along the way. I want to express my gratitude to my students first of all. I teach the course Introduction to Pastoral Ministries at Indiana Wesleyan University, which is designed to help students understand the ministry and the call. While writing this manuscript, I have had the privilege of leading more than a hundred freshmen through this course, and they have read, reacted, and shaped the manuscript considerably.

Several colleagues in the academic community gave me considerable help in reading and correcting the manuscript. Dr. Steve Lennox, who faithfully read each chapter as quickly as I wrote it and returned his input. Dr. Bud Bence and Ken Schenck supplied always-insightful ideas upon reading a chapter. Dr. Bob Black of Southern Wesleyan University provided invaluable insights and improvements on the manuscript.

Elizabeth Glass gave me excellent advice on the approach to the chapter on women in the ministry, along with Mandy Hontz Drury, who gave input on the entire manuscript. My wife, Sharon Drury, was a constant advisor and willing reader of the manuscript, even though she was right in the midst of her doctoral work.

Finally, I wish to thank two persons at Wesleyan Publishing House: Larry Wilson, for his excellent editing and improvement of the book, and Don Cady, for his publishing vision and constant prodding for me to continue writing, though I have especially focused my own life's ministry on mentoring students. Without these two, this book would never have come into being.

KEITH DRURY
February 12, 2003

When people speak of being called into the ministry, what do they mean? What does a minister actually do all day? We see them up front on Sundays, but what do they do through the week? Is the ministry interesting work? What do ministers like most about it? What do they like least? Is this something I might like to do?

what is the ministry?

this book is about the ministry—not so much the general ministry that every Christian should be doing, but *the ministry* as a vocation or life calling from God. This ministry is a lifetime vocation of helping God's people—the church—grow, develop, reach out, and worship Him.

The ministry is a job, but it is much more than a job. It is also a profession like law or medicine. It is an established occupation with its own vocabulary, way of thinking, and generally accepted code of professional conduct. Yet the ministry is more than a profession, it is a *vocation,* a calling.

The ministry is a wonderful way to spend your life if God lets you. While few ministers get famous and fewer get rich, there are far greater rewards than money or fame, rewards that last through all eternity. It is almost impossible to find an older minister who doesn't think his or her life was wonderfully meaningful. Go ahead and ask several! Ask them if they regret going into the ministry, and if they think their life was well invested. Almost every one of them will say "I'd do it again in a second." Of all the things you could choose to do with your life, investing it in the ministry might just provide the greatest possible satisfaction. If God calls you to it, you'll love the ministry as a vocation.

> investing your life in the ministry just might provide the greatest satisfaction

it's hard but it's worth it

However, don't get the idea that the ministry is a cushy job without trial or difficulty. It isn't. Ministry today might be one of the toughest professions you could consider. As a minister, you will be called to lead a congregation of people who have widely differing opinions and preferences. They will want church to be like a fast food restaurant where they can order exactly what they want and receive it in forty-six seconds.

In many denominations, the people you'll lead will also be your bosses; they might get to vote on keeping you as their minister or even "vote you out" so that you have to go to another church. In business, if you are dissatisfied with employees you can fire them; but you can't fire church members (although in many cases they can fire you!). And people, being what they are, can sometimes get downright nasty. Often, it's the minister who bears the brunt of their displeasure.

And there is competition. There will be dozens of other churches down the street from you who will offer better programs, bigger screens, and more exciting and relevant music. Sometimes people leave one church and move to another. It hurts when people leave the church you lead, yet you can't hold your congregation at arm's length and say "It's just business." It's hard to not take rejection personally.

But the real competition isn't from other churches. All Christians are really on the same side. The real competition comes from the Devil. If you started a business, you might face stiff competition from other businesses, but the Devil is not likely to spend much energy trying to run you out of the hardware trade, for example. The Devil focuses on the church with his evil, competitive program. He'll try to drive your church out of business and you out of the ministry. In fact, that may be the Devil's chief work on earth! The minute you accept a call to the ministry, you will have a bull's-eye on your chest.

The ministry is more fulfilling than it is easy. It's hard work, but it's worth it. It's a bit like running a marathon, where you sweat more than the bystanders and hurt more than the spectators. Your muscles ache and scream for you to give up. There's no doubt about it, the ministry can be tough at times. A marathon runner never likes the pain in her legs, yet she still runs because finishing the race is a worthwhile goal. And of course, even an aching, sweating runner gets a "runner's high" during the race. Ministers get lots of ministry highs, but even on the days when it doesn't feel particularly good to be a minister, they keep going because they believe ministry is a worthwhile and eternal pursuit. When you cross the minister's finish line, you'll know that it was worth it! If you are called to the ministry, you aren't promised an easy life, but you are promised a life that's worthwhile.

> if you are called to the ministry, you aren't promised an easy life, but you are promised a life that's worthwhile

what does a minister actually do

Knowing the daily work of a minister will tell you a lot about what you may like or dislike about this calling. But be careful: you shouldn't enter the ministry simply because it sounds like fun or is a good career fit. It takes more than a vocational test to send you into the ministry. It takes a clear call from God that is confirmed by the church. If you enter the ministry, do so because you are called by God, not because it fits your personality or personal likes and dislikes (more on *the call* in a later chapter).

To help you get an accurate idea of what ministers actually do through the week, here is a summary of the general types of work that they do.

church work

Ministers work with the church—the body of Christ on earth. God is at work in the world mostly through His church. The church is the place where Christians gather for worship, evangelism, discipleship, and service. No, God is not limited to the church, but He does most of His work in and through it. That is His plan to reach and change the world. The vast majority of ministers are associated with a local church. Even so-called parachurch organizations (like InterVarsity, Campus Crusade, or Young Life) could not exist without the support of local churches, and the people who work in such organizations are full participants in local churches. The local church is at the center of God's plan to win and disciple followers, and bring His kingdom to pass here on earth. Sometimes the local church falls short of God's vision for it, but it is still His primary means for accomplishing His plan in the world. While there are some jobs in ministry that are done completely outside the local church, almost all ministers do work that is in some way connected with a local congregation. If you don't like the local church, don't go into the ministry; that's where most ministers spend their career.

people work

Ministers work with people. All the time. In fact, when ministers get into trouble, it's usually because they don't get along with people rather than because of some immorality. God's ministry is to serve God's people, so if you enter God's ministry you'll be working with His people most of the time. You may start the day at a breakfast meeting to plan an upcoming event with someone from your church. Then you might go to a staff meeting at church where you'll coordinate plans for the day and week. Next, you might have several appointments with people, scheduled back to back, about all kinds of things; some might be serious problems, others might be routine administrative matters. After that, you might go to lunch with parents who have some questions about how to handle their teenage daughter during a difficult time. That afternoon you might have some quiet time for study and prayer. And what will you pray for? People! After dinner with your family, you might go to an evening committee meeting, or to a church service, or maybe to a counseling appointment with a couple who are planning to get married. People, people, people!

Ministers spend a lot of their time with people. If you are called into the ministry and don't like people, start praying now that God will give you the only gift that will sustain this much people work: love. The work of the ministry is mostly people work.

pastoral care

Consider this day: A high school athlete snapped her anterior curciate ligament and was taken to the hospital where she's about to find out that her senior year of soccer is washed up. An old woman living alone fell and broke her hip yesterday and wasn't discovered until this morning. Her children live two states away and don't know yet. A young couple in the church had a baby last night but the newborn child is on a respirator because "something went wrong." A man and woman who've been married ten years have been arguing so fiercely that they are considering a divorce; calling you is their last ditch effort to keep their marriage alive. There are two aged church members, great saints of the church, who are now in nursing homes and seem to be forgotten; few people visit them. A fifty-five-year-old man was given a pink slip when he showed up at the factory this morning. He'd

> when life begins to fall apart people look to God for strength and consolation. the minister is often the primary representative of God to these folk

worked for the same company for thirty-five years and now has no idea how he'll pay his daughter's college bill. His wife just called you.

All of these people have one thing in common: they all want *you*. Well, not exactly you. They want God, but they consider you to be the closest thing to Him. When life begins to fall apart people look to God for strength and consolation. The minister is often the primary representative of God to these folk. If reading the list above made your heart hurt—you felt a bit of compassion for those hurting people—good for you. If you had no response at all yet feel sure that you are called to the ministry, begin asking God to share His compassion with you. He does that. But if you have no plans ever to be with hurting people in times of crisis, then the ministry is not for you. The work of the ministry includes giving tender pastoral care to hurting people.

worship leadership

Laypeople see their minister most during worship. Some think leading worship is all we do! While a minister has plenty of other duties, leading worship is certainly one of the most wonderful. Planning and leading worship provides the greatest job satisfaction for many ministers. Even if you serve on the staff of a church and don't get to preach or even say anything during worship, this event is usually the high point of the week for most ministers. Here we get to see the people of God gathered to give their praise and hear Him speak. A minister's job almost always includes learning how to plan and lead worship.

preaching

Ministers represent the people to God and God to the people. They represent the people to God through intercessory prayer, sacraments, and other rituals, but they represent God to the people by reading Scripture and preaching. When a minister preaches, he or she speaks for God by delivering a *message* from Him. It is a scary task at first—and always. Just like the ancient prophets, a minister sometimes encourages, affirms, and comforts the people. At other times the preacher corrects, chastens, or even scolds the people.

	Prayer		Preach	
GOD ↔	Sacraments	← **YOU** →	Affirm	→ **PEOPLE**
	Rituals		Correct	

So how does the minister know what to say? God's words have already been spoken in the Bible. A minister seeks God's guidance to determine which part of the Bible speaks to *this* church, *this* week, through *this* minister. He or she does this by both assessing the people's needs and by listening to God through prayer. Youth ministers do this with teenagers. Senior pastors do it with the entire church. Other staff ministers may get to preach only occasionally, but whenever they do, they speak for God, not just for themselves. That is the difference between a *speech* and a *message*.

teaching

The pastor is the chief Bible teacher in a local church. All Christians need to know what the Bible says, what it means, and how it applies to life today. Ministers teach them. Ministers often teach Sunday school classes or new member classes, and most teach some sort of mid-week Bible study or class. Some who are especially adept at it even teach during worship services along with preaching. Even if you have a staff assignment that doesn't include preaching, it will probably will include lots of teaching.

rituals

Consider these stories: Kara and Jeremy are engaged and have planned a church wedding for this Saturday. Dan and Laura just had a baby girl and want to dedicate their child to God this Sunday. Alex, Faith, Craig, Tammy, Jamie, and Paul all came to faith in Christ during the past month and are prepared to be baptized this week. Agnes passed away Monday and her funeral will be held at the church this afternoon. This coming Sunday is also the first Sunday of the month, the day this church usually offers communion.

Each of these occasions—and other milestones in life—is marked by one of the sacraments or rituals of the church. These are symbolic actions that help people celebrate,

ministers help people move from one stage of life to another

grieve, or process some spiritual event. Ministers officiate such rituals, helping people move from one stage of life to another. Pastors are often ministers of transition. It is some of the happiest work a minister gets to do.

evangelism

All Christians have a responsibility to spread the good news about salvation, but ministers have a special burden to see lost people come to faith in Christ. When asked about the most satisfying aspect of ministry, many will cite "leading people to faith in Christ" or "watching people grow in their faith." All ministers get the opportunity to do this. They even get paid for it!

Mark, chapter 9, tells the story of a blind man who stopped Jesus beside the road and asked to be healed. How would a blind man have known that Jesus was about to pass by? The story doesn't say, but probably someone told him. That's our job. We don't have to restore sight, that's God's job. And we can't save anybody; that's God's job too. Our job is simply to announce His arrival.

> ministers disciple, provide accountability for, and mentor leaders in the church

discipleship and mentoring

Ministers are generally appointed to serve an entire community of people, but they spend plenty of one-to-one time with people also. Ministers disciple, provide accountability for, and mentor leaders in the church. When college students are asked to list the people who have had the greatest impact on their lives, ministers are named far more often than their number within the total population would suggest.

administration

A minister is not just a preacher but is often a church's CEO as well, managing the sprawling programs of a local church. Administration includes things like making budgets, conducting meetings, writing letters, doing paperwork, recruiting people, organizing events, calling people on the phone, and gathering facts. This "office work" is a part of ministry, just like pastoral care. While some ministers don't particularly like this part of their job, they do it because it is necessary to keep the church moving. Many ministers, however, see administrative work in a better light. They consider administration to be their greatest act of service, since it is usually done behind the scenes and brings little praise, but is necessary. Either way, ministers tackle administration with a joy "as unto the Lord."

leadership

Every Christian should minister to others and serve the church. But the ministry is not just getting paid to do what every Christian is supposed to do anyway. It is more than being a full-time Christian. Ministry is leadership. It is helping the people of God discover what God wants them to do, then organizing them to accomplish it. The minister's job is to call out and equip Christians to do their work.

This is one reason we ordain ministers. God calls ministers but the church ordains them. When we do that, we are saying that this woman or man is anointed by God as a leader. That doesn't mean that ministers can act like kings and boss everybody around. We do not need any more pastor-as-master types in the church. But we do need more pastor-as-servant leaders, ministers who recognize that the privilege of leadership must be used to serve the best interests of the people. Ministers are called to lead the people of God in discovering and fulfilling His vision for them. So even if you do not consider yourself a leader, when you are in the ministry, people will look to you for guidance. Ministry is leadership.

community relations

A minister is God's representative to the people. Primarily, that means that he or she represents God to a local church. But ministers have a similar role in the communities in which they live. Ministers cannot collapse their sphere of influence to fit exclusively within the congregation. They relate also to the entire city or town. The minister is a community leader, not just a local church leader. The minister represents his or her church to the community by serving on boards, organizing events, and sometimes even by running for elected office. A minister can go few places—especially in a smaller town—without being recognized as "the pastor," a representative of his or her church. That relationship works both ways. A minister also must represent the needs of the community to the congregation, serving as a sort of go-between for the community and the church.

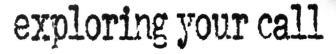

exploring your call

to share

1. Of all the things that ministers do, which two do you feel most nervous about doing yourself?
2. Which ones do you most look forward to doing?

to discuss

1. How do you think the work of the ministry could change in the next twenty years? How might we keep ourselves current so we won't become ineffective or out of touch?
2. This chapter proposes that the ministry is "hard but worth it." Do you think some ministers have it easier than others? Is there any way to avoid the unpleasant parts of the ministry? How?

to do

1. Interview an experienced minister and make a list of ways that their work has changed over their lifetime. Ask about what they do more, less, or differently. Ask about what they do that is new or what they have stopped doing.
2. Make a chart of the ministerial activities listed in this chapter, then rate yourself from 1 to 10 for each activity, based on your present abilities and interests. Pick the two strongest activities and list ways you might leverage these strengths even now, as you prepare for ministry. Pick the two weakest abilities and list ways you might improve in both.

Is there any difference between the ministry a pastor does when visiting a sick person in the hospital and the ministry a factory worker does by visiting that same person? When we say that a minister is called to the vocation of ministry, do we mean that nobody else can do their work? What does it mean to be ordained? What is the difference between general ministry and equipping ministry?

the difference between ministry and the ministry

what is ministry

did you ever tell a restaurant waiter or waitress "Thanks for ministering to me"? It sounds strange, doesn't it? But the work that a waitress does can be described by the term *ministry*. The root meaning of that word is *to serve*. It's the same word we might use to mean simply waiting on tables at a restaurant. Ministry is serving others.

> ministry, at its most basic level, means serving others

At its most basic level, ministry includes everything any person might do to serve another, from bringing food, to counseling, to holding elected office, to operating a drill press at an automobile plant. Each of these jobs provides a service and meets a need for others. In this broad sense, everybody is a minister, including Christians, Muslims, Buddhists, and atheists. Ministry is service, and every person in the world can do that.

what is christian ministry

Christians often use the term *ministry* in a more specific way to denote service that is itself Christian either in content or in motivation. Service that is Christian in content is that which helps a person develop a Christian lifestyle or values. Leading a Bible study is one example of that. The content of the act is Christian, so it is Christian ministry.

service that is christian in either content or motivation is christian ministry

Service that is Christian in motivation has more to do with the attitude of the person who does it than with the act itself. Any service offered out of a Christian motivation can be Christian ministry. When a Christian stops to help a person stranded on the highway because he believes that "this is what Christians do," it is Christian ministry. In that sense, Christian ministry might include anything from helping to build a Habitat for Humanity house to picking up trash on the

the terms the ministry and Ministry usually refer to the ordained profession of the clergy

road in front of one's own home—if these things were done as a Christian duty. Thus, two people might work side by side to provide flood relief services—one a Christian and the other an atheist—and the only one of them would be engaged in Christian ministry. It is even possible for two *Christians* to serve beside each other with only one of them acting from a Christian motivation.

So Christian ministry is any service to others that has either a Christian motivation or is Christian in content. This is sometimes called the *general ministry*. Every Christian is called to this sort of ministry.

what is *the* ministry

Most churches use the term *the ministry* to describe the profession of a pastor who is called to a full-time church vocation. You might hear some pastors say, "All Christians are called to ministry but some are called to *the* ministry."

Others make this distinction between the general ministry of all Christians and the specialized ministry of pastors by capitalizing the word *Ministry*.

Interestingly, this means that pastors are called to two kinds of ministry: the general ministry to which all Christians are called and the professional *equipping* Ministry in which clergy spend their professional lives.

what is equipping ministry

The *equipping ministry* is the same thing as *the ministry*. It is simply another term some churches use to mean ministry as a profession. The term comes from the Bible, which tells us that God gave the church apostles, prophets, evangelists, and pastors and teachers to "equip the saints for works of ministry" (Eph. 4:12 KJV). This means that people who are called to the ministry are given the task of preparing other Christians for the general ministry that they will do in their regular jobs, at school, at home, or wherever they are. Ministers have the job of preparing and training laypeople to do their own ministries. Thus, every Christian is called to be a minister, but God sets apart some to equip the rest.

> equipping ministry is the job of a pastor or other minister, preparing laypeople for general ministry

what is the call to ministry

While it can be said that the Bible calls every Christian to evangelize, disciple, worship, and serve others, some Christians receive a personal call from God to minister as a profession—to give their entire lives to the ministry of equipping other Christians. We sometimes use the phrase "called to full-time Christian work" to describe that experience, and we may ask, "Have you been called to the ministry?" The call to the equipping ministry is not something you apply for; it is something that is bestowed upon you. Such a call does not make you better than Christians who have received the general call to ministry, but being called to the equipping ministry has always been recognized by the church as a special call from God to serve and lead His people. This double use of the term *call* can cause some confusion, but it is not unlike some other professions in which the terminology has a dual use. For instance, anyone may counsel a friend who is facing difficulty, but some people study in order to enter the vocation of counseling. Everyone—especially parents—teaches sometimes, but some people enter the vocation of teaching. Any of us might nurse our spouse or child when they get sick, but some people are nurses by profession. Likewise all Christians minister, but some are called by God into the vocation of the ministry.

what is ordination

Ordination is the rite the church uses to set apart a man or woman for a lifetime of equipping ministry. In most churches it is a solemn ritual done only after many years of education, training, and examination and several years of ministry experience in a local church. In most denominations, ordination is irrevocable. If a minister falls morally,

> the *call* is God's recruitment of christians into the ministry as a lifelong profession

his or her license to practice ministry might be taken away and locked up in some denominational vault. But even if that minister is later *restored* to ministry, he or she is not re-ordained. A person can only be ordained once. In this, most Protestant churches are very much like the Roman Catholic church, which says, "once a priest always a priest." Ordination is the church's recognition of the minister's lifetime authority to represent God to the people and the people to God.

> ordination is the rite by which the church sets apart a priest or minister for lifelong equipping ministry

Ordination is a serious matter and should not be pursued for light or temporary reasons. Roman Catholics take ordination so seriously that they consider it to be a sacrament. Protestants do not consider it a sacrament, but hold it as one of the most important nonsacramental rites. Though few use formal titles today, ordained persons were traditionally referred to as "the Reverend So-and-so." In many denominations, only ordained ministers may perform marriages, preach regularly, preside over the Lord's Supper, or perform baptisms.

what is nonordained ministry

This book is not about church jobs. This book is about the ordained ministry.

Almost all churches hire an ordained minister as their leader, though some churches—particularly large ones—also hire people to work as nonordained employees. Generally, those people might be hired as lay Christian education directors, secretaries, lay youth workers, janitors, or worship leaders. Notice that many of these jobs could be done by either an ordained or an nonordained person. For instance, an ordained person who worked with teens would be called a youth pastor. A person doing the same work as a layperson might be called a youth director. It's the same with worship: an ordained person whose job is leading worship is usually called a minister of worship while a nonordained staff person in a similar role might be called a worship director. Though a nurse and doctor do similar things—and even do the same things sometimes—they are not the same and we use different terms to describe them. Doctors have much more training, authority, and far greater

> ordained ministers have greater authority and responsibility in the church, though there are also many nonordained jobs that people can do to serve the church in full-time general ministry

responsibility than nurses do, though either one might be hired to do certain jobs at a hospital. It's the same in the church.

Although many denominations have ten times as many jobs for ordained ministers as for nonordained staff persons, there are still lots of church jobs for laypeople. One of the early decisions you will need to make if you sense a call to ministry is whether you feel a lifetime call to ordained ministry—with all of the rights and responsibilities that it implies—or simply feel drawn to doing church work as a nonordained person.

These terms may seem confusing, but it's important to understand the difference between the general ministry of all Christians and the specialized role of ministers in the Ministry. This book deals specifically with vocational Ministry. It is addressed to those people who sense an inner conviction that God has called them to the work of being a prophet and priest for His people. When that call is confirmed by the church, they will be ordained for lifelong ministry and most likely serve the local church in one way or another.

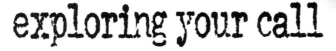

exploring your call

to share

1. Tell about a time when you did ministry that was Christian in motivation, though not content.
2. Describe someone you know who is hired to work on the staff of a church but is not an ordained minister.

to discuss

1. How can those who are called to the ministry make it clear that they don't think they're better than the average layperson?
2. What are the reasons that most people who work on the staff of a church are ordained?

to do

1. List the terms used in this chapter along with a simple definition for each that will be easy to remember.
2. Write a single paragraph weaving together all these terms that explains the basic message of this chapter.

What does it mean when we say a person is called into the ministry, or called to be a pastor? How can I know for sure I am called (or not called)? What do Christians mean when they talk about a "calling"?

what is a call to the ministry?

e could study a variety of definitions of *the call* to the ministry, but let's settle on this one: The call to ministry is an inner conviction from God, confirmed by the church, that I am commissioned to lifelong, vocational service as an equipping minister for the people of God.

Let's take a look at each part of this definition so we can understand what it really means to say that someone is "called into the ministry."

understanding the call

an inner conviction from God

While the call comes in a variety of ways (see chapter 5, "kinds of calls"), the result is always the same: I become inwardly convinced that God is calling *me*. This conviction may begin gradually, and at times it may be stronger or weaker, but the call itself is my inner confidence that this indeed is what God wants me to do with my life. The call might have external signs or outward confirmations, but the call itself is inner; it is in my heart where God speaks to me. As God prompts and prods my heart, my "inner ear" can increasingly hear His quiet voice convincing me that He really does want me to devote

the call is an inner conviction from God, confirmed by the church, that I am commissioned to lifelong vocational service as an equipping minister for the people of God

my life to the ministry. As I listen to God's prompting I will probably take some baby steps in response to His call. As I take these initial steps, I will become increasingly convinced of the certainty of this call. Eventually this certainty will rise to the level of a conviction. I will be completely convinced this is what God wants me to do. In fact, this conviction will be so strong that I'll know it would be wrong for me to pursue any vocation other than the ministry. This is the call to the ministry.

One of the confirmations of a call is its growing nature. An authentic call gets stronger, not weaker over time. But the call does not grow in clarity all by itself. A call grows clearer as we respond to what we've already sensed. For some, the call tumbles in like a thunderbolt from the sky, but for many men and women it comes gradually, starting with a tiny hint or *precursor* from God. Once this hint comes, it is our turn to respond. We might respond by taking a volunteer job at church or starting to give devotional talks at a nursing home. Once we begin to respond to God's initial call, He often turns up the volume of His inner voice. When we respond to that increased volume by taking even more ministry opportunities (like going on a missions trip, or starting some courses in ministry), God's voice becomes still stronger and clearer. It's true that some people are called to ministry instantaneously and have that call confirmed immediately, but most others move through several years of this "dance" with God. He whispers the next move, and we respond. Over time, His whispering gets louder, and we keep responding until we become completely convinced that we have a calling from God.

But what happens if you respond to what you thought were God's hints of a calling but you do not get an increased conviction that you should be going into the ministry? What if you feel *less* convinced over time? It works both ways in this case. Those experiences may be the confirmation that you are *not* called to the ministry. That's why it is so important to get involved in some ongoing church ministry immediately upon sensing the first hints of a call. As you respond to what you believe is God's call, He will confirm it one way or the other. If you get involved in ministry for a couple of years, your conviction will become more certain—either more certain that you are called or more certain that you are not. This inner conviction won't increase as you sit around and wonder about the future. It almost always comes only as you experience the work of ministry.

The call, however, does not come from the work itself but from God. It is an inner conviction *from God.* There are no vocational tests you can take to tell you what God is saying to your heart. Vocational tests are helpful for determining whether you might be well suited to the work of ministry—just like reading this book will do that—but they can't tell you for sure whether God is calling you personally. You have to find that out by listening to God's voice, then responding by doing more ministry until the call becomes *an inner conviction from God.*

confirmed by the church

But your call is not just between you and God; it involves the entire church, the people

> as you respond to what you believe is God's call, He will confirm it one way or the other

of God. How can you know for sure that you are not just wishing yourself into the ministry? How can you know if the voice you hear is truly God's or just your grandmother's? You can know this by getting either confirmation or blocking from the body of Christ, the church. This is the primary way God will confirm your call. He will prompt His people to see your gifts and graces and affirm them, thereby confirming your call. If you think God has called you into the ministry but you find no church willing receive your ministry, then you should seriously question your call. God confirms the call through the body of Christ. If you sense a call to the ministry and get involved in a church, you may hear God's people affirm that call. The church's ultimate confirmation of your call will be your ordination service, during which the church will set you apart as a minister and leader for life. A call is an inner conviction from God that is *confirmed by the church.*

leading to a commission

Conviction is your inner certainty that God has said "Come, I want you to do My work." *Confirmation* is the church's affirmation of your gifts and graces. It is the body of Christ saying "Yes, we think God has called you." But that's not all there is to a call. A call also includes a *commission*.

> the call to *the* ministry is an inner conviction that God wants me to serve Him for life as a professional minister

The term *commissioned* means *sent*. God commissions people to the equipping ministry: He *sends* them to His church. Equipping ministers are God's "gift" to the church (see Eph. 4). So a call to the ministry includes a sense of being sent, or commissioned, to serve the church. To be called is to become convinced that God is sending me to do His work.

for lifelong service

God recruits people all the time. He recruits people for salvation. He recruits people for service. He recruits people to live a holy life. He even recruits people for specific tasks He wants done. So we can honestly say that God is recruiting everybody all the time. In fact, God calls everybody to ministry, the general ministry whereby all Christians are supposed to meet the needs of others. But the call to *the* ministry as a lifetime vocation is different. It is an inner conviction that God wants me to serve Him for life as a pastor, youth pastor, or other professional minister. It is the conviction that I am to spend my entire life—my vocational life, my profession, my daily job, what I do for income—in church work. Having a call from God to the ministry is to know what I plan to do for the rest of my life. It is a call to minister and build up God's people.

The origin of the term *vocation* may help in understanding this. The term comes from the Latin words *vocatio* (summons) and *vocare* (to call). In the fifteenth century, the term was used only to describe the call into the priesthood or a religious order. At that time, the only people who had a vocation were priests and members of a religious order. Everyone else simply had a job. Gradually, the term vocation was broadened to include every kind of work that a person might do as a full-time occupation, and the notion arose that all Christians should consider their work as a life calling, whether it was in the church or in a factory. But when we speak of the call to the ministry, we are speaking of a lifelong vocation. Having a call means spending my entire life in the ministry.

as an equipping minister for the people of God

The ministry to which you are called is not just to serve needy people, though it includes that. The ministry is about equipping God's people so that *they* can serve others by doing ministry. Equipping people involves empowering and leading them. We use the term *equipping ministry* to distinguish this calling from the general ministry that all Christians should be doing.

What does an equipped congregation look like? Equipped people are actively involved in teaching Sunday school, serving on missions teams, supporting the church financially, serving the needy, evangelizing, establishing justice and mercy in society. If you are called, you are God's gift to the church: He gave that gift to help others grow and develop into mature believers. You will minister both as a prophet and as a priest. As a prophet, you will speak for God by preaching, teaching, and providing wisdom. As a priest, you will represent the people to God by leading rituals, interceding in prayer, and leading praise.

The classic Scripture for understanding the relationship between a professional minister and the people is Eph. 4:11–13.

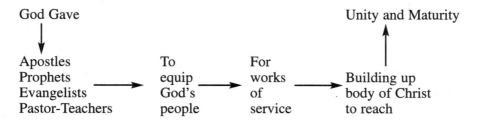

A call to the ministry is a call to work with people. It is not a calling to run off as some sort of lone ranger, disconnected from God's church. Rather, God calls apostles, prophets, evangelists, and pastors and teachers so that they can equip God's people. Ministers prepare people for their own lay ministries. They do this through teaching, advising, counseling, preaching, and by all the other activities a minister does.

Why equip the people? Ministers equip God's people to minister to each other so that the people of God will come to the unity of faith in the knowledge of Christ. When that happens, the church will become "mature, attaining to the whole measure of the fullness of Christ." The call is an inner conviction from God, confirmed by the church, that I am commissioned to lifelong vocational service as an equipping minister for the people of God.

common misunderstandings about the call

There are some prominent misconceptions about the call to ministry. Many people are familiar with what the call *is*; perhaps it would be good to discuss what it *isn't*. Here are some things that are *not* true about the call to ministry.

misunderstanding one: everybody is called

This idea has been mentioned several times already, but it's such a deeply rooted misconception that it deserves one more pass. While it is true that God calls everyone to minister to others, to do what they can to serve those around them, God does not call everyone into professional ministry as a lifetime vocation. God has always selected men and women to serve as priests and pastors, representing God to the people and the people to God. So while all Christians should do their work as if they were doing it for the Lord, that doesn't necessarily mean that God wants them to enter the lifetime vocational ministry of equipping and leading His church.

> while it is true that God calls everyone to minister to others, God does not call everyone into professional ministry as a lifetime vocation

God has chosen no other plan to accomplish His will on earth but His church. A life in business is exciting and worthwhile, but Christ was not the cornerstone of Wall Street; He was the cornerstone of the church. A career in Hollywood might be exciting and a great opportunity to affect the world's value system, but the martyrs did not shed their blood for the film industry, but as the soil from which the church would grow. Inventing better ways to reduce harmful effects on the environment and conserve the beauty of creation would be a wonderful—and Christian—way to spend one's life, but

Christ did not die to save trees but human souls from destruction. None of this is to say that these or other jobs are not meaningful ways to spend one's life. They are. But God has chosen to establish His church as the primary means of accomplishing His will, His primary way of bringing in the kingdom of God to earth. As good as the Sierra Club is, it was not established by Jesus Christ. As wonderful as the United Way is, God did not found it on that first Pentecost. The call to the ministry gives us the chance to work with God's primary tool of doing His work on earth, the church.

It is true that God gives everyone personal direction about their lives, and that direction might include their career choice. So, in a sense, a person could say "God called me to be a doctor." But that is not a call to the ministry as we understand it. The call to the ministry is a call to the lifelong service of equipping the church, and not everyone is called to do that.

misunderstanding two: only one type of person is suitable to be called

Some people mistakenly assume that God only calls one type of person to the ministry, a person who "fits the mold." Perhaps they have known a particular minister who was very effective and conclude that only someone like him or her could be a pastor. Or maybe they only attended huge churches and assume all ministers should have personalities like the superchurch pastors they knew. Such folk might think that your personality isn't suited for the ministry and scoff at your call.

> some people mistakenly assume that God only calls one type of person to the ministry, a person who "fits the mold"

But they would be wrong.

Such people would never have approved of Moses as a leader of God's people; not only did he stutter but he was also guilty of killing a man in a fit of anger. God looked past Moses' lack of communication skill (and even his past sin) when He called him to lead the Israelites. In fact, God seems to enjoy using weak people; "But God chose the foolish things of the world to shame the wise; God chose the weak things of the world to shame the strong" (1 Cor. 1:27).

Ministry jobs are as varied as the culture and size of a church. There are huge suburban churches that want one type of pastor while small rural or inner-city temples may want a totally different kind of minister. There are senior pastor jobs and staff pastor jobs. There are ministry jobs working with adults in nursing homes where you would dress and act conservatively, and there are ministry jobs working with young people where you might paint your face blue and wear a baseball hat backwards when you preach. There are ministry jobs that involve planting new churches that meet in living rooms, and there are jobs working with children. There are churches that want a quiet, unassuming, humble pastor, and there are churches that prefer an outgoing, talkative person who seems more like a salesperson than a minister. There is no cookie-cutter personality profile that fits all ministry types. God's church is too varied.

> most ministers have received their call more quietly and less dramatically than by an audible voice or a sign in the sky

When God calls a woman or man into the ministry, He has a place for that person to serve, even if she or he does not fit the mold of what others think a minister should be like. When God calls a person, He has a ministry in mind. God knows what He's doing.

misunderstanding three: the call always comes as an audible voice

Perhaps the most common misconception of the call to ministry is that it comes in an audible voice or through a clear sign from God. Sometimes God does use miraculous signs or confirmations to call a person to the ministry, but the average call is far less dramatic. Most ministers have received their call more quietly and less dramatically than by an audible voice or a sign in the sky. A lack of drama should not equate to a lack of certainty. It is important to not compare your own calling with another person's; likewise, it is crucial to keep from judging another person based on your own experience of being called. The person who falls in love gradually is not less certain of his or her affection than the person who falls in love at first sight. Both experiences can lead to certainty. And both falling in love and hearing God's call must both lead to an *inner conviction* that is *outwardly confirmed.*

misunderstanding four: the ministry is a human, not a divine invention

Some Christians say there should be no distinction between a layperson and a vocational minister. They say that everyone is a minister and that the role of a pastor or priest was invented by human beings, not God. They think every believer should act as his or her own priest and that the church needs no leadership other than the Holy Spirit. The only trouble with that advice is that God has never followed it. Throughout history God has selected men and women for His service. A vocational minister stands at the front of a long line of called people—from the Old Testament, through the New Testament, and right up until today.

And that's what the next chapter is about.

Read @ the Library
@ 67th St. bet 1st & 2nd
February 13, 2004
4:52 p.m.

exploring your call

to share

1. Share your own sense of calling on a scale of 1 to 10, with 10 meaning absolute certainty and 1 meaning barely exploring a call.
2. Describe the most effective minister you have known in your life so far. What was he or she like? What actions or attitudes made this minister effective?

to discuss

1. Aside from the ones listed in this chapter, what are some other misconceptions about being called to the ministry that you have encountered?
2. In Eph. 4, Paul says that "God gave" equipping ministers to the church. This book is mostly about pastor-teachers. Do you think the other categories of ministers—apostles, prophets, and evangelists—still exist today? If so, what do you think they do?

to do

1. Do a Bible study on being called to the ministry by looking up the term *call* and making a chart that lists the best examples of the general call and of the specific call to equipping ministry.
2. Make a diagram of the definition of *calling* described in this chapter to make it easier to remember. You might make it similar to the diagram of Eph. 4 that is given in this chapter.

Is this idea of a special call to the ministry something new or does it have biblical and historical support? Is being a priest or minister a recent invention? If I am headed into the ministry, who will I look to as role models, both from the Bible and throughout history? To whom can I look to for guidance about what it means to be in the ministry? What exactly is my ministerial family tree?

the minister's family tree

no matter where you are in the world, you will find religion. And within every religion you will find a class of people who serve as priests, ministers, or leaders of some kind. These religious leaders serve the function of bringing the people and God together. Put most simply, the priest or minister represents God to the people and the people to God.

Christianity holds this in common with other world religions. As Christian ministers, we have a long line of ministers and priests in our family tree. While ministering in the present day is certainly more important than digging up the roots of our ministerial family tree, it is worthwhile to know our ministerial lineage. We do not accept a call to the ministry lightly. We join an impressive line of people who represented God to the people and the people to God long before we were born.

Many of the following titles overlap, which reminds us that God always raises up spiritual leaders to meet the needs of His people in a particular place and time. The job titles and descriptions may have shifted some over the generations, but God always calls spiritual leaders to minister to His people.

Here is a review of the major categories of leaders that God has called throughout history. As you read this list, you'll probably see some similarities between each of these job descriptions and the present-day role of a pastor. But you'll notice some differences too. The minister's role today is really a composite of all these functions.

the patriarchs

The patriarchs did not have a minister; they *were* the ministers. Abraham, Isaac, Jacob, and Job dealt directly with God. They had no synagogue, no temple, no priests, and not one scrap of the Bible. As the head of the household or tribe, each patriarch served as the clan's priest. Sometimes they also represented God to the people outside their clan. Noah, for example, represented God to a corrupt world, providing an escape for anyone who might have repented. Abraham interceded on behalf of the city of Sodom, representing its citizens to God.

> when you are ordained, you will pick up the mantle of the patriarchs as you pass on God's message to your people and intercede for them

The patriarchs, however, were not completely without other priests. While Abraham felt competent to officiate at his own sacrifices, he still paid a tithe to Melchizedek (Gen. 14:17–20). Melchizedek was *a priest of Salem* (the city later known as Jerusalem). Presumably, Melchizedek was a local priest who represented God to the people and the people to God. Remember that all of this took place long before there were any temples or even the Ten Commandments. So while the Patriarchs were do-it-yourself priests, at least one of them, Abraham, related to yet another priest, Melchizedek.

When you sense a call to the ministry today, you can trace your vocational lineage back to these patriarchs. Our family tree includes all the patriarchs and

Melchizedek. When you are ordained, you will pick up the mantle of the patriarchs as you pass on God's message to your people and intercede for them.

moses

The ministry of Moses made a transition from the patriarchs to the priests. Here's how it happened. Jacob's son Joseph had been sold into slavery by his brothers and was shipped off to Egypt. Joseph's entire clan eventually joined him there, where they were first treated as honored guests but later enslaved. Hundreds of years passed, and Moses became the leader of the combined clans, who came to be known as the children of Israel (Jacob's other name) or *Israelites.*

> when you are ordained, you will take up the mantle of moses, speaking for God to the people and interceding for the people to God

When the call came to Moses, he had been living with a man who was called a "priest of Midian." Moses returned to Egypt in order to lead the Israelites out of slavery. Moses became a sort of super patriarch, the spiritual and administrative leader for an entire people. God had called Moses to lead the people not just militarily and politically but also *spiritually.* Moses represented God to the people as he received and presented the Ten Commandments as their rules for living. The first five books of the Bible, the Pentateuch, are referred to as the Books of Moses. These books contain God's detailed instructions for His people. These were not God's instructions just to a single person, such as God gave to Abraham when He told him to sacrifice his son Isaac. In the Books of Moses, God spoke to all the people Moses represented.

Moses also represented the people to God in his prayers and intercession for them. Just as Abraham had interceded for the people of Sodom, so Moses was the mouthpiece for the Israelites before God. Do you remember how he begged God to spare their lives?

When you are ordained, you will take up the mantle of Moses, speaking for God to the people and interceding for the people to God.

priests and levites

But Moses was not a solo priest for long. His brother, Aaron, emerged early in the story as a kind of grandfather of all priests. After the Israelites were led out of Egypt, a portable church called *the Tabernacle* was constructed where collective worship and sacrifice took place. This was not just for families, as had been done in the past, but for an entire nation of people. One particular tribe of that nation, the Levites, was called to serve as priests and assistants to the priests. These *priests and Levites* of old became ministers not by being individually called but by being *born*. It was an inherited calling. If you were born as the son of a priest or Levite, you were called to be a priest or Levite. When Israel worshipped, the priests and Levites guarded the Tabernacle and officiated at the sacrifices.

When you are ordained you will take up the mantle of the priests and Levites as you lead worship and officiate the sacraments of baptism and communion, conduct rites like marriages, child dedications, and funerals.

judges and kings

When the Israelites finally entered the Promised Land, they lost Moses and were ruled to some degree by judges. Later, Saul became the single national king, initiating the monarchy in Israel. These judges and kings were primarily military and political leaders, yet some had a spiritual leadership function as well, especially David the second king of Israel, and his son Solomon, who constructed the first Temple in Jerusalem. Some later kings like Hezekiah were priest-kings. The priests and Levites still officiated at the Tabernacle and later the Temple, but the judges and kings provided some spiritual leadership.

> you will take up the mantle of the priests and levites as you lead worship, officiate the sacraments, and conduct rituals

When you are ordained, you will take up some of the mantle of administrative leadership from the judges and kings. This administrative function is now focused mainly on managing the church, though some ministers get involved in local or national political leadership.

the prophets

Wouldn't you think that having a king to look out for the political and spiritual welfare of the people, plus priests and Levites to conduct worship, would be enough? It wasn't. God raised up another class of representatives called prophets. In fact, prophets actually originated before kings, since Samuel preceded Saul, the first king of Israel. Samuel was called to represent God to the people as both a priest and prophet. He anointed Saul, and later David, as king. By that act he indicated God's selection and approval of the leader. Samuel stands at the beginning of a long line of prophets.

But who needs them? Why did God designate this new class of representative? Weren't the kings and priests enough? Apparently not. As leadership within the nation of Israel became increasingly specialized, it appears that the existing leaders focused mostly on their primary tasks. That is, the kings focused on political and military leadership more than spiritual leadership. The priests and Levites focused especially on representing the people to God by officiating at Temple worship and sacrifices. But who would represent God to the people? Who would not just conduct worship rituals but also speak for God? God raised up the prophets to do this.

The prophets wandered about speaking God's word to the people, sometimes scolding them or making predictions of disaster, other times encouraging and heartening them. They were ancient preachers. You might have noticed that today's worship services often include two parts: the *upward* elements of praise and prayer, which are directed from the people to God, and the *downward* elements of Scripture and sermon, which are directed from God to the people. The prophets specialized in this second part: presenting God's word to the people. Thus we have a long series of books in the Old Testament produced by these fiery preachers, people like Isaiah, Jeremiah, Ezekiel, Daniel, Hosea, Joel, Amos, Obadiah, Jonah, Micah, Nahum, Habakkuk, Zephaniah, Haggai, Zechariah, and Malachi.

When you are ordained you will take up the mantle of the prophets, preaching God's word to the people, even when it is not popular.

scribe

The scribes studied and copied the Word of God, the Torah. They were students of the Scripture and carefully transmitted it to the people. The scribes are not directly in our line of ancestry—they're something like cousins—but they do represent the careful study of Scripture and the urgent desire to propagate the knowledge of God's written Word among the people. That's something that all ministers are concerned with.

> you will take up the mantle of the scribes in your commitment to study and propagate the scriptures in your own heart and in the lives of your people

When you are ordained you will take up the mantle of the scribes in your commitment to study and propagate the Scriptures in your own heart and in the lives of your people.

rabbi

A rabbi is a teacher. Ancient rabbis gathered around them people who were interested in study. These people were called *disciples.* Jesus was a rabbi, and He gathered and taught many disciples. When you are ordained, you will take up the mantle of the rabbis, for you are called not only to manage the church and preach but also to teach your people.

synagogue elder

The primary place of worship in the Old Testament was the one national Temple in Jerusalem, but by the time of Jesus, the Jews also had a multitude of gathering places very much like local churches. These were called *synagogues.* Probably developed during the period of Babylonian captivity as a means of preserving and passing on the faith, the synagogue was introduced to Israel after the release from exile. In a synagogue, a congregation of Jews gathered to pray and read and study the Scriptures. The synagogue was the local place of prayer and Bible study for Jews during the time of Christ. The size of the town dictated the organization of a synagogue. If there was one rabbi, he would be the synagogue ruler. In large synagogues, there may have been a college of elders presided over by a person known as the chief of the synagogue, a sort of president or presiding elder.

When you are ordained, you will take up the mantle of the synagogue ruler as you either lead a congregation solo or perhaps join the staff of leaders at a larger congregation.

apostle

Jesus had lots of disciples. From that large group of followers, He called out twelve to serve as *apostles*. These twelve formed Jesus' inner circle. They were His designated successors, to whom He gave authority to multiply the church and make decisions in His name. He even promised that they would do greater things than He did!

After Christ ascended into heaven, the apostles took up the job of leading the church. Since their authority had been given to them by Christ Himself, they were very much respected and obeyed without much question in the early church. They also received Christ's commission to make disciples. Eventually, they took the gospel from Jerusalem to Judea, Samaria, and to the uttermost parts of the world.

> you will take up the mantle of the apostles by exercising authority over Christ's church and by assuming responsibility for Christ's commission to make disciples of all nations

When you are ordained you will take up the mantle of the apostles by exercising authority over Christ's church and by assuming responsibility for Christ's commission to make disciples of all nations.

deacon

At first the apostles did everything—including distributing food every day to the widows in Jerusalem. But after a while, they realized that they were spread too thin and that their focus was too broad. Moses had a similar experience centuries earlier. His father-in-law, Jethro, had confronted him saying, "The work is too heavy for you; you cannot handle it alone" (Exod. 18:18). Both Moses and the apostles eventually accepted help from others. In fact, God prompted the apostles to develop a new class of church workers called *deacons*. (At first, they were simply called "the Seven," because there were seven of them.) These workers took on the management of food distribution so the apostles could give themselves whole-heartedly to prayer and the ministry of the Word.

These days, most evangelical churches have position titles like *trustee* or have deacon boards composed of laypeople who handle the building maintenance, construction, or compassion ministries, freeing the pastor to focus primarily on preaching and teaching. Some denominations ordain deacons as a second class of ministry. In others, deacons work is considered lay ministry. Either way, when you are ordained you will take up the mantle of the deacons too for much of the modern pastor's work in managing and organizing the church is really deacon's work.

prophets and teachers

In the church at Antioch there were *prophets* and *teachers*, which were New Testament versions of the Old Testament prophets and rabbis. They preached and taught the people, developing strong Christians who had a strong faith. Paul and Barnabas belonged to the group of prophets and teachers.

The prophets presented the gospel with authority and sometimes warned people about disobedience, occasionally foretelling future events and even chastising people as the Old Testament prophets had done. They were, in a sense, preachers. The teachers trained and built up the people so they would be strong and solid in the faith. Together they made a great tag-team approach the ministry.

When you are ordained you will take up the mantle of both the prophet and the teacher as you answer God's call to both preach to and train the people.

bishop or overseer

Originally, a *bishop* was probably the chief pastor of a local church, something like a senior pastor would be today. Eventually, the bishop became a regional church leader, supervising other ministers and churches. The work of a bishop still exists, and the job still carries that title in some denominations. Others use terms like *district superintendent* to describe this role.

When you are ordained you will take up the mantle of the bishops even if you never become a bishop, district superintendent, or general superinten- dent in your denomination. For in the modern world, every minister exerts a significant influence over other ministers and thus serves as a trainer and improver of his or her colleagues.

elder

Local spiritual leaders in the New Testament church were sometimes called *elders*. Some denominations still refer to their ministers as *ordained elders*. Elders presided over a congregation and were looked to for wisdom and guidance. At first they were probably older than most of the others, but even if they were just mature for their years, their wise leadership was respected. The elder presided over the church service and was thus referred to sometimes as the *president*. When you are

> every minister exerts a significant influence over other ministers and thus serves as a trainer and improver of his or her colleagues

ordained you will take up the mantle of the elder, for even though you may still be young, others will look to you for wisdom and insight.

widows

The early church had a special category for *widows*; they were something like the first nuns in the church. Specific instructions were given for these women for a house-to-house ministry (1 Tim. 5:9–11). When you are ordained you will take up the mantle of the widows, for you will not be able to "go to work" at the church building all the time. Your ministry to people will take you from house to house as well.

apostles, prophets, evangelists, pastor-teachers

Paul listed four categories of equipping ministry in Ephesians, chapter 4, repeating some of the above list but adding two not mentioned yet: *evangelist* and *pastor-teacher*. The job of an evangelist may have been to travel from church to church in order to reach the lost and spread the good news of the gospel. The pastor-teacher was most likely the local elder given care of the flock to teach and train the people in obedience. When you are

most ministers have received
their call more quietly
and less dramatically than
by an audible voice or
a sign in the sky

ordained you will take up the mantle of the evangelist as you do the work of winning the lost; and you will take up the mantle of the pastor-teacher by becoming attached to one group of people and committed to training them in godliness.

at the end of a long line

As an ordained minister, you will stand at the front of a long line of people whom God has set apart to build the church. Your family tree is a wonderful one. There are thousands who have gone before you, serving God and His people by representing the people to God, and God to the people. To know those who have gone before us helps each of us be faithful to the calling. What a great heritage we ministers have!

exploring your call

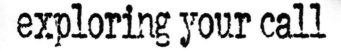

to share

1. Of all the roles listed in our ministerial family tree,
    which is most attractive to you? Why?
2. Tell about a minister you know by comparing his or her work to one
    of the categories from the tree. You might begin something like this:
    "He's mostly like an elder because . . ." or "She's most like an evan-
    gelist because . . ." or "She's kind of like a priest because. . . ."

to discuss

1. Over time, God seems to keep changing the way He calls ministers,
    the work that they do, and the titles they have. Why might God do
    that? Do you think God might change these things again in the future?
    How?
2. Is it important for us to use the same terms that the first century
    church did? If so, which of the biblical terms should we use to
    describe the ministry?

to do

1. Make a chart organizing all branches of the ministerial family tree.
    Make one column for the terms and another that describes the work
    involved.
2. Make an actual family tree that displays the ministerial heritage
    described in this chapter. Include all of the limbs and branches right
    up to today's ministers—and you.

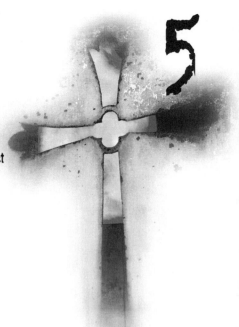

So how does God's call to the ministry come to a person? Do all people get called in the same way? Is one sort of call better than another? How are most people called to the ministry today?

kinds of calls

through all of history God has called men and women to stand in the gap, representing the people to God and God to the people. He still calls men and women to do this today. The way God calls people has varied throughout history and is often different from person to person. God calls people on a case-by-case basis, so no two calls are exactly alike, but there are at least five identifiable ways in which the call commonly comes to people today. Or perhaps we might say five ways one *recognizes* the call.[1]

---

[1]I am indebted for this paradigm of the kinds of calls to the work of Dr. Lee M. Haines and Dr. Bud Bence.

the damascus road call

The *Damascus Road call* is certainly the most dramatic and impressive, even though most of the ministers who are called today did not experience this kind of call. There are several examples of this type of call, both in the Bible and throughout Christian history.

the apostle paul

The Damascus Road call is named after Paul's conversion and call (The apostle Paul apparently was converted and called at the same time). The story is told in Acts, chapter 9. Paul was on his way to Damascus to persecute Christians when a light from heaven flashed around him. Paul was thrown to the ground and temporarily blinded, and Christ spoke to him directly. When Paul told the story at his trial (Acts 26), he said it was then that God called him to go to the Gentiles to spread the gospel. A bright light from heaven? The voice of Jesus? Knocked to the ground? Blinded? It took a lot to get Paul's attention!

the way God calls people has varied throughout history and is often different from person to person

Which makes sense. After all, he believed the Christians were a dangerous sect that ought to be stamped out as quickly as possible. People like this seldom recognize a call gradually!

isaiah

Another person in the Bible experienced a call like Paul's—Isaiah (Isaiah 6). Isaiah was in the Temple when he had a vision of God's presence that included seraphs, earthquake-like shaking, coals from the altar, and smoke. He heard the voice of God asking, "Whom shall I send?" Isaiah responded by volunteering: "Here am I Lord, send me." God answered with, "Go and tell this people. . . ." Vision of God? Foundations shaking? Seraphs? Smoke? The voice of God? This is certainly a Damascus Road call.

charles finney

One of the most famous Damascus Road calls from recent church history is that of Charles Finney. He was a lawyer who started reading the Bible because he had been employed by a church to defend it in a lawsuit. While Finney was praying in a grove of trees, God called him in a dramatic way that transformed his life. He dropped his lay practice saying, "I have accepted a retainer from the Lord Jesus Christ to plead His cause."

things to remember about this call

The Damascus Road call is a dramatic event whereby a person clearly and unmistakably hears God's call to the ministry. The Damascus Road call usually is accompanied by a sign, a miracle, or an unmistakable manifestation of God's voice. If you have had a Damascus Road call you will have no doubt about your call to the ministry. You know *for sure* that this is what God wants you to do, and you remember the experience vividly. But there are some things to remember about this type of call.

God Doesn't Call Everyone This Way. Most of us would prefer a Damascus Road call. It would be so certain, so clear, so definite. But God does not call every person into His ministry in the same way. Perhaps some need such a call because they wouldn't listen to God's inner voice. Perhaps God knows it takes a powerful whack to get some people to pay attention. Who knows? What we do know is this call is relatively rare today; perhaps as few as 10 percent of those called into the ministry experience it. If you are fortunate enough to have a Damascus Road call then you have no choice. Into the ministry you must go, with no doubts or questions.

The Non-Damascus Road Called Need a Caution. Those of us who have a less dramatic call often ask God to make it clearer by speaking to us in an audible voice or giving us an obvious sign. This is OK as long as we do not try to tempt God by forcing His hand to prove something to us. The practice of "putting out a fleece," like Gideon did, can be a risky way to discover God's will. As we shall see, God usually confirms His call with a clear and certain voice, but this voice is often an inner, inaudible voice, not an external, audible one. Speaking in an audible voice accompanied by lights, smoke, earthquakes, seraphs, or blindness is not God's usual mode of operation. God alone will choose when and how He will give confirmation of your call; it is not for you to demand it.

There Are Benefits to Not Having This Call. People who experience a Damascus Road call are minding their own business, headed from point A to point B, when Bam! they get called. A person who does not experience Damascus Road call often goes from point A to point B, then on to points C, D, and E until they arrive at a point of certainty about God's call. Why is this beneficial? Although the road might have been a little longer, they usually pick up lots of knowledge and experience along the way. The journey is part of the training. And the biggest lesson is often the need to constantly listen to God's voice and to continue relying on His guidance at every stage.

> God usually confirms His call with a clear and certain voice, but this voice is often an inner, inaudible voice, not an external, audible one

the progressive call

The *progressive call* does not come as a thunderbolt but as a growing certainty. The result is the same: the individual becomes absolutely sure that God has called him or her into the ministry. It is probably the most common type of call today.

like the dawning of a day

This call comes like the dawn, gradually and progressively until it is finally no longer night but day. Long before the sun rises, the sky begins to get less dark. First the eastern sky becomes a dark gray, then a light gray, then almost light until, finally, the sun rises above the horizon. A progressive call is like that. A person might sense a precursor to the call long before he or she is certain. Gradually, the call gets more sure until the "sun rises" and there is a bright certainty that God has indeed called this person to the ministry.

Sometimes the progressive call begins when a person discovers that God has given him or her the gifts needed for ministry. Seeing the need for these gifts in the church, that person begins serving, which leads to a greater sense of certainty about the call.

like falling in love

Many people fall in love and get married this same way: progressively. Sure, there are some people who walk across a college campus, spy a guy and wow! they know immediately that this is The One. But most folk do not have such a Damascus Road love life. Most of us fall in love gradually, over time, with a growing certainty, until, finally, our love grows to the point that we know for sure we want to spend our entire lives together, then we "pop the question."

questioning the progressive call

Those who receive a progressive call often go through phases of questioning or even doubting their call. Some people even get cold feet the night before they are to be married. Likewise, women and men with a progressive call may have some uncertainty even on the day before they are ordained. When people with a progressive call hear stories of others who received Damascus Road calls, they yearn for similar certainty about their calling.

Yet we have to believe that God knows what He is doing. He works with each of us according to our needs. So who are we to dictate how God will call us? It's His job to decide. If you have a progressive call, focus

> a progressive calling forces us to keep an ear to the ground—an ear attuned to the inner voice of the Holy Spirit

on God's persistent and growing inner voice—is it getting stronger? Who knows, perhaps if you had a Damascus Road experience you might be tempted to run forward on your own. A progressive calling forces us to keep an ear to the ground—an ear attuned to the inner voice of the Holy Spirit.

the call from birth

There are a few ministers who cannot recall a time when they *weren't* called. They were called either at birth or before. These ministers came to realize and accept their call very early in life. In fact, some came to accept it so early in life that they can't even remember a time when they weren't called. The *call from birth* has existed in every era of history, but it is very rare.

jeremiah

Jeremiah tells us he was set apart and appointed to be a prophet before he was formed in the womb (Jer. 1:5). The ministry was his destiny before he was even born. Thus, for Jeremiah, it was not so much hearing God's call, but *recognizing* the call that was already on his life.

samuel

It might be said that Samuel was prayed into the ministry. Before his mother had even conceived, she prayed, "O LORD Almighty, if you will only look upon your servant's misery and . . . give her a son, then I will give him to the LORD for all the days of his life" (1 Sam. 1:11). Before Samuel could even move inside his mother's womb, he may have been set apart for God's service.

discovering your call

If you have never known a time when you weren't called, you may have a call from birth. Some ministers argue that all calls fit into this category. They reason that since God has already determined whom He will call, the called person does not so much hear the call as discover it. Even if you have another type of call, this notion is worth considering, for it may shift your mind-set about the whole idea of being called. On the other hand, it may be that God's actions are more fluid—that He watches the battle rage and calls up soldiers and officers for His army to fit with the progress of the war.

People with a call from birth sometimes struggle with doubt because they wonder if they "caught" their call from parents or relatives. They wonder if their call is really a result of environmental influences, not God's doing at all. Since they have never considered anything else for their lives, they sometimes want to explore alternatives when they get to college, before coming to certainty. But if they were indeed set apart from birth, they almost always return to their original calling with more certainty than ever. If you have a call from birth, thank God that you were so sensitive as a child that you heard His inner voice early in life.

the set-apart-by-the church call

How does God speak? Through His Bible, most of all. But not everyone who reads the Bible is called to the ministry. He speaks personally to individuals by a prompting or inner voice. Sometimes that happens during Bible reading, of course, but the voice of God generally comes to us one-to-one, as individuals.

God also speaks through other people, especially through the body of Christ, the church. Occasionally God uses the church to call people to the ministry. They may be set apart for service by the church even before they sense a personal call. This is the *set-apart-by-the-church call.*

barnabas

Perhaps Barnabas fits this category. He first appears in the Bible as a solid Christian who sold a piece of land and gave the proceeds to the apostles (Acts 4:36). The apostles in Jerusalem then set him apart for a special mission: to check on the Gentile revival in Antioch (Acts 11:25). He recruited Paul to join him, and the church in Antioch eventually set Paul and Barnabas apart for ministry and sent them out on the world's first missionary journey. Here the church (first the apostles in Jerusalem, then the leaders in Antioch) *set apart* and *sent out* Barnabas as a missionary.

the church must always confirm a call, even if it has been received privately and personally

Some people first realize that they might be called when older Christians in their local church urge them to consider a call. This is one example of the way God sometimes speaks through other people, especially His local body of Christ. After all, who would you trust more to discern the voice of God: an individual or a group of committed believers?

Ambrose is another example of the set-apart-by-the-church call. Back in the fourth century, he was a provincial governor and layperson who was swept into the office of bishop by popular demand—and against his own desires. Yet he was an effective bishop and later led Augustine to the Lord.

the corporate element

The set-apart-by-the-church call comes when God speaks through the body of Christ, His church here on earth. Sooner or later, the recipient of such a call will want personal certainty about his or her call. That will most likely come through the same inner voice heard by people with a progressive call or call from birth.

It's important to remember, too, that *all* calls have a corporate element. The church must always confirm a call, even if it has been received privately and personally.

identifying your call

Sometimes a person can't hear God's voice as well as others can. Perhaps a saint who has walked with God for fifty years can sense what He is saying better than you can. God will sometimes use such a person, or a group of such people, as a mouthpiece. If a minister or dear saint in your church has urged you to consider whether or not you have a call to the ministry, you might be hearing a set-apart-by-the-church call. But just because people think you ought to go into the ministry won't be enough for you. You'll have to add your personal certainty to their affirmation. The set-apart-by-the-church call may be the way that you begin to hear God speaking.

the open door call

An *open door call* happens when a person who has ministry gifts finds an opportunity for ministry, an "open door" of ministry. They walk through it, and their fruitful ministry leads to yet more ministry opportunities until they come to sense that God is calling them to do this very work for the rest of their life.

mission trips

This often happens to young people on missions trips. They experience a high water mark of ministry, and while they are seeing fruit multiply, they sense that this is exactly what they should do with their life. It is not the situation that calls them, but while they are in the situation, after walking through the open door of ministry opportunity, they come to hear God's call.

close association with a pastor

This sort of call also happens to people who come to be closely associated with a pastor or other local church ministers. It is particularly common among PKs (preacher's kids). Such young people get plenty of opportunities to see what ministry really is like. They have early occasions to serve, lead, and speak. They witness the remarkable fruit of ministry: changed lives, a loving sense of community, and people helped in their growth toward Christlikeness. While they are in the midst of that atmosphere, they sense God speaking to them: "This is what you should do with your life." While this call may be combined with other kinds of calls, it is very common among young people who are closely associated with ministry at an early age.

An open door alone does not make a call. But when we step through it, God sometimes speaks to the heart, convincing us that He indeed does have a call for our lives.

a combination call

If you were to ask a hundred ministers about their call, you would discover that most can't fit their experience into just one of the above categories. They would likely say that their calls were a combination of several kinds. God is a God of infinite variety, and His call comes to people in many ways. For a few it may come as an audible voice or sign. For others it may come progressively as a growing inner conviction. For still others it may come first from other people in the church or even through an open door of ministry experience, being confirmed later by an inner conviction. But for most, it comes in a combination of several of these ways.

> God is a God of infinite variety, and His call comes to people in many ways

Regardless of how it comes, the call to ministry is an inner conviction from God confirmed by the church that I am commissioned to lifelong vocational service as an equipping minister for the people of God. Eventually, the called person must be able to say *with certainty*: "God has called me." There may be times of equivocation or doubt, and the call may be stronger or weaker at some times, but over time, if you are truly called, your inner conviction will become a certainty. By the time you are ready to be ordained it will be a lifetime certainty. You will know this is what God has planned for you.

exploring your call

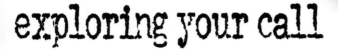

to share

1. If you are sensing a call to ministry, tell your own story, relating it to one or another of the kinds of call.
2. Do you know the story of anyone else who was called to the ministry? Share it.

to discuss

1. Do you think God changes the way He calls people according to the culture and expectations of the day? That is, when the culture expects more dramatic calls, does God accommodate that expectation?
2. Perhaps it would be better to speak of the *ways we hear* God's call rather than about different kinds of calls. It could be that all calls really amount to the same thing, an inner certainty of God's commissioning. If that's true, can you think of some other ways in which a person might begin to hear God's call?

to do

1. Interview an active or retired pastor and get the story of how he or she became sure of the call. Be able to tell that story to others.
2. Make a drawing or chart that gathers the content of this chapter in a visual way on a single sheet of paper. Include both the kinds of calls listed and your own insights about them.

How can you know for sure that you are called? Is there some test you can take or guide you can follow that will make it perfectly clear? What if a person thinks he or she is called but the church doesn't think so? Exactly how does God confirm a call?

confirming your call

nearly everyone who is called to the ministry wonders at some point whether they really are called. We all look for—and need—some *confirmation*, something from the outside that confirms what we believe to be God's inner voice. And we ministers are not the only ones who need that confirmation; the church also must be sure that we are called. That confirmation will come in several ways.

mystical confirmation

Many calls to ministry are not dramatic in themselves, but most calls have a *mystical confirmation* of one kind or another. Mystical confirmation may be either a mysterious outward sign or a spiritual inner certainty. If you are truly called, there will come a time when you are certain—*absolutely convinced*—that you have a definite call from God to enter the ministry.

Sometimes this mystical confirmation comes as a *sign* or as a response to a *fleece*, such as the one Gideon set out before the Lord. In other cases, it comes in a moment of supernatural, inner surety, a moment when one realizes, "This is exactly what I will do with my life." It is sort of like a Damascus Road confirmation. Even if the call itself was progressive and gradual, the confirmation of that call may come in a single dramatic moment.

> mystical confirmation may be either a mysterious outward sign or a spiritual inner certainty

Although ministers may receive a mystical confirmation in different ways, almost all ministers have a story of the time when they "knew for sure" that they were called to the ministry. Consider these examples:

Steve: I walked out of the dorm and it was like I walked through a curtain. On one side I was not sure of my future and on the other side I knew the ministry was my destiny, no matter what.

Nathan: I was praying and it tumbled in on me as clear as if someone had spoken—though I heard no voice—I said "I'm going to be a preacher." And as soon as I said it I knew this was true. It was settled for life.

Heather: In my women's Bible study one young Christian said, "You ought to be a pastor" and another immediately agreed. Then three more said, "Really, we're serious. It is obvious God is calling you." That night I woke up at 2:00 A.M., and it was like a sweet presence was all around me. I just knew. I knew for sure that I had to quit my job and go get the training I needed to become a pastor. So I did.

Eric: I was reading Romans and had been looking for either confirmation or a blocking of a call, and my eyes fell on Rom. 10:13–15. The words "how shall they hear without someone preaching" leapt out at me as if God were speaking them directly to me. I knew at that moment that the ministry was to be my life forever.

In each of these accounts, a person who may have sensed a gradual call to the ministry came to an immediate, mystical, spiritual certainty about it. Some receive that certainty early in their preparation—or even before it begins—while others received it later, but most ministers receive it somewhere before ordination. Such certainty usually comes in a mystical way even though it may not have any signs or miracles attached to it. This mystical confirmation is something like our assurance of salvation. How do we know *for sure* that we are saved? The same way we know for sure that we are called: by God's Spirit bearing witness with ours.

You may not be able to prove scientifically that this surety is from God, but you nevertheless *know for sure* after that point. This is mystical confirmation. There are some ministers who never have received this certain confirmation yet are ordained and active in ministry, just as some people get married though they are not totally sure about their decision. Most denominations, however, expect you to come to certainty before taking your ordination vows. No matter what your denomination requires, it's OK for you to seek certainty about your calling from God. If you do not find it, seek advice and counsel from your denomination's ordination board or committee.

If you have had a mystical confirmation already, thank God for this certainty. If you have not had it, continue to seek confirmation until you receive it. Just as you can know for sure that you are really a Christian, you can know for sure that God is calling you to the ministry. Until you receive this certainty, accept the other confirmations that come your way, some of which are explained in the remainder of this chapter.

> just as you can know for sure that you are really a Christian, you can know for sure that God is calling you to the ministry

church confirmation

While the mystical confirmation of your call is personal and individual, the church's confirmation is public and corporate. In fact, the primary external confirmation of your call will come through the church, the body of Christ on earth. If you are called to the ministry, one of your early steps should be to associate with a local church and ask for their approval to begin preparation for the ministry. A local church, after all, is where you will be ministering and leading. How could you possibly be a minister to people who do not accept your ministry? Sooner or later your denomination or local church will decide whether to ordain you to the ministry. The first step toward this ultimate church approval is your association with a congregation that can assess your potential for ministry and guide you in your preparation for ministry.

How will a congregation confirm that you are called? They will examine your life. They will want to hear your testimony of how you became a follower of Christ. They will ask you why you think you are called so they can hear your story. This will not be a hostile interrogation but a helpful time of getting a "third witness" to your call-

when an entire congregation decides that you are truly called, it is a more powerful confirmation than your own feelings

ing. Until now, your call has been between you and God; when you approach the congregation for their confirmation, your call becomes a church-wide matter. The church will take its first step toward affirming your call when they approve you as a candidate for ministry training. They might even support your preparation financially as a further evidence of their affirmation. And they will always pray for you.

We can't simply say "God called me, I know it, so you have to ordain me." While God does speak to individuals, He also works through His church to confirm or correct what individuals think they've heard from Him. There's safety in numbers. When an entire congregation decides that you are truly called, it is a more powerful confirmation than your own feelings, which rise and fall at times.

In addition to examining your character, testimony, and sense of calling, the church will also examine your *gifts* and *graces*—your abilities and aptitudes for the work of ministry. They will try to determine if God has gifted you with the ability to do this work. They won't be looking for perfection; nobody will expect you to be an ideal minister at this stage. But they will look for promising signs that you have the capacity for ministry. They'll try to determine whether you are gifted in evangelism, teaching the Bible, leading people, and other areas in which a minister needs skill.

They will look at your graces—your aptitudes, preferences, and personality—to see if you are a suitable person for ministry. One grace they will search for is your likeability. A person who is obnoxious and doesn't like people lacks an important grace of the ministry. Another grace is hospitality. Hospitality means receiving people in a friendly way, taking people along with you, being inclusive.

There are dozens of other gifts and graces, but for now, know that your denominational board will help you discover and develop the attributes that are important to your future. To help them do that, some ministerial training boards use career tests and interviews along with checking references. A career test can't tell you that you are called for sure, but it might point out special challenges you would face in the ministry or areas you need to develop. Some training boards administer a battery of psychological tests too, not to keep people out of the ministry so much as to help them resolve issues that could be a detriment in the future. Meeting with your denomination's board or committee will be a helpful thing for you.

When the church says *Yes*, approving you for ministerial preparation, you should consider it the greatest confirmation you have received up to that point, at least equal to any other personal, inner feeling or outward sign. If the church says *No*, it is a gigantic blockade to your ministry future, at least in that denomination. If they say *Wait*, it is worth pausing to examine your call, or at least letting it marinate for a while.

Confirmation from the church will probably become the single most important confirmation of your call. When Christ's church on earth says, "Yes, we believe you *are* called to the ministry, and we will support you in preparing," you have solid evidence that you really are called. All other confirmations are precursors or add-ons to this greatest-of-all confirmations.

confirmation by desire

If you are called into the ministry, your desire to be a minister should increase as time goes by. You should *want* to be a minister, perhaps not always at first, but more and more as the years pass.

There is a dreadful notion around some youth groups that God delights in calling people to do what they hate doing. They imagine that God is just waiting for someone to say, "Well, I'd never want to be a minister" then *Bam!* He knows exactly whom to call next. What kind of God would that be? Certainly a capricious and fickle God like that would not deserve our service! God doesn't get workers by choosing only those who don't want to do the work. And He isn't out to make us miserable by placing His calling on our life. Rather, He calls us to do the work in which we will be most satisfied and fulfilled.

That doesn't mean that God always calls us to do what we are best at. People with that wrong notion in their heads begin by thinking about themselves and assume God's goals are centered on them personally rather than on His mission to reach the world. Every person—not just future ministers—should ask where they can best further God's kingdom. The career question is not "How can I make the most money?" or "What job would make me happiest?" It isn't even "What am I naturally best equipped to do?" The career question for all Christians is the same: "How can I best further the kingdom of God, given the aptitudes and skills that I have?"

God sometimes calls people to the ministry who could easily become millionaires or be successful, even famous, in some other line of work. In the ministry, these gifted people might never get either wealth or fame. In fact, they may not even be great ministers, just ordinary people, but obedient ones. So the place to start is not yourself, but with something greater than you, the kingdom of God on earth.

While God occasionally calls people who feel unworthy or ill prepared (Moses is a great example of that), He does not simply look for people who don't want to be called, then call them. Even if you had no desire to serve as a minister when you were first called, God will give you an increasing desire. Over the years, your desire should grow, not diminish. It is one of the confirmations of your call. If you think less and less about the ministry and want less and less to spend your life in it, you should seriously question your call. If, as you prepare for the ministry, you gain a greater desire to do it, that is a confirmation that God has called you.

firstfruits as confirmation

It is imperative that any person preparing for the ministry get involved in some form of ministry now, even as they prepare. Most men and women start ministering while they are in training. In fact, doing ministry is an important part of the preparation for the ministry. You will do this too. You might volunteer to speak at a nursing home, lead children's church, teach a Sunday school class of eighth graders, or go on a missions trip. Have you done some of those things? If not, and you think you may be called to the ministry, start doing some ministry soon. As you serve, God may confirm His call by letting you see fruit—the *firstfruits* of your ministry.

- If you speak at a nursing home, you may notice an old woman with a tear in her eye. Then, as you sit at her bedside, she may tell you how much your devotional encouraged her heart.

- If you lead the children's church, you may have parents tell you, "My daughter is so excited about the Bible stories you tell every week." Or one day in children's church, several children may pray to receive Christ.

- After you teach the eighth-grade Sunday school class, one boy's father may tell you, "My son used to hate to go to Sunday school, but now he tells us about it every week. His life is changed!"

- On a missions trip, you might discover that your influence has an impact not only on the people of a foreign country but also on your teammates, who were influenced toward godliness and obedience by your presence even though you never led a public service.

In each of these cases you would be experiencing the firstfruits of your ministry, lives that were influenced for God and changed. Since you can't change lives with your own power—only the Holy Spirit can do that—seeing change in other people as a result of your ministry is a giant confirmation of our call. If you remain involved in ministry, you will likely

even if you had no desire to serve as a minister when you were first called, God will give you an increasing desire

73

see increasing fruit and thus increasing confirmation of your call. Are these fruits an indication that you are a wonderfully gifted minister? No. They are signs that the Holy Spirit is a wonderfully gifted minister and has chosen to work through you. Your job is not to produce results. Your job is to be obedient, to be the channel for the Holy Spirit's power.

Like all confirming signs, however, this one is a double-edged sword. It could be that you will get involved in ministry and never see any results; God will give you no fruit. Nobody's life will be changed, nobody will be receptive to your ministry, and nobody will be influenced for God's sake through your service. If so, you should start questioning your call. While there have been great missionaries who served for years (and sometimes decades) without fruit, generally speaking there is some positive result from the ministry of those who are truly called by God. This is why the examining board of your denomination will ask you about fruit, not just about your call, gifts, and graces.

> somewhere along the line, something is going to happen that will make you question your call and maybe even doubt it completely

confirmation by testing

If you are called by God, you can expect your call will be tested. Somewhere along the line, something is going to happen that will make you question your call and maybe even doubt it completely. That test might be a barrier that seems insurmountable, like not being accepted into the only college to which you applied. Or a test may come when someone important to you scoffs at your call. A test might come when a minister you looked up to falls morally. A test might come when the person you have fallen in love with announces that he or she has no intention of marrying a minister. The test might come when you observe a minister going under attack for making changes in a congregation and you wonder what you're getting into. Perhaps the test might come as an inner doubt, feelings of uncertainty or inadequacy, or a sense of spiritual inferiority.

Testing can come in a variety of ways, and it can come from several sources. When you are tested, it may be that Satan is trying to get you to abandon your calling. After all, do you expect him to stand by and let you zip into ministry without placing a single obstacle in your path? Or it may be that your test will come from God Himself—just seeing if you will respond in obedience despite the problems or the cost. The testing might even come from yourself, especially if you are a contemplative person who often overreflects and questions yourself frequently.

Whatever the source, God can always use testing as a confirmation of your call. He even puts the Devil's attempts to discourage us to a good use. How? Testing reveals the depth of our inner conviction about the call. An untested call is a shallow call. But a call that has been clung to over time, even in the face of trial or doubt, will be strong. Thus a time of testing can make you give up on a call, or it can serve as a powerful confirmation of your call. So if you are called, expect that call to be tested, perhaps several times throughout your life, and know that these tests will be opportunities for you to deny your call—or confirm it.

So how do you get confirmation or blocking of your call from God? *Do something!* God will seldom confirm your call while you are sitting still. Start seeking clear assurance from God in a mystical way. Connect with a local church to see if they will affirm your call. Ask yourself whether your desire to minister is increasing or shrinking. Get involved in ministering to others to see if fruit is produced. Open yourself up to testing and see if it strengthens or weakens your inner conviction.

God guides us best while we are moving. So start moving and see if God confirms or blocks your call. He isn't trying to make this hard for you. If you are called, He certainly doesn't want to keep it a secret or make you play Pin the Tail on the Donkey to find His will. Seek clarity from God, and He will respond. But don't just sit on your hands waiting. Do something!

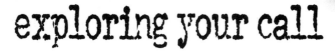

exploring your call

to share

1. If you sense a call to the ministry, tell about any experiences of mystical certainty that you've had to date.
2. Scribble out a line graph, like a stock market chart, illustrating your own certainty or uncertainty about your call to ministry so far. Include the ups and downs that you have experienced from the time you first considered your call until now.

to discuss

1. Do churches ever make mistakes? What should a person do who is certain he or she is called but cannot obtain the church's approval to prepare for ministry? What should a church do when it has serious doubts about a person who says he or she is called?
2. How can you tell the difference between a testing of the call that comes from the Devil and one that comes from God? How would you know the difference between a testing from God and a blocking of the call from Him? That is, how would you know whether God was trying to test your commitment to the ministry or keep you out of it?

to do

1. Contact your denomination's office (or visit its web site) to determine the procedure that your church uses to confirm a call to ministry. What are the "hoops" you will need to jump through on your way to ordination, occasions when the church will check on the things mentioned in this chapter?
2. Make a chart including the six confirmation factors from this chapter, and journal your own experiences of and reflections on each factor up to this point in your life.

What if you are a woman who has sensed a call to the ministry from God? Can women be ministers? Can they be ordained? Or is the ministry reserved for men only? What if you are a woman and you are called to the ministry but your denomination won't ordain women? Is it biblical for churches to ordain women? Didn't the Apostle Paul say women should be silent in the church?

women in the ministry

t his chapter is for women called to the ministry; however, men should read it too. Does your denomination refuse to ordain women? You should still read this chapter to see why some denominations do ordain women. Does your denomination enthusiastically ordain women? Read this chapter to see why some denominations resist the idea. Does your denomination rarely (perhaps even grudgingly) ordain women? Then you especially should read this chapter to determine how you might influence your church in the future. You might not agree with this chapter, and your denomination might not either. But whatever your views, you should read this because it will cause you to think seriously about this issue.

the bible and women in the ministry

Whole books have been written about what the Bible says about women in the ministry, and probably more books will be written. This brief chapter will not attempt to recount all of the arguments for and against women's ordination that claim to have biblical support. Eventually, you will want to read a few of those books to get a more in-depth understanding of the biblical arguments that underlie this debate. What this chapter will do is provide a brief survey of both positions. Of course, these summaries are not perfectly representative; there are as many viewpoints on this issue as there are colors in the rainbow. But generally, these two summary statements will help you understand the primary positions. They are not presented so you can bash the "other side" but to help you understand both ways of thinking and, eventually, build a bridge between the two.

Don't worry; the church will come to general agreement on this question just as we did several hundred years ago on the issue of slavery. At that time, many churches argued that slavery was clearly supported by the Bible. Yet some used the same Bible to claim that slavery was wrong. The quarrel took years to resolve. Eventually, the entire church of Jesus Christ, worldwide, came to agreement on the issue. This will happen concerning women's ordination too; but probably not until many more years pass. In the meantime, understanding the positions, processing the subject, and arguing (in a Christian way) are the best things we can do to help God's church move toward consensus. For starters, here is a summary of the two primary positions.

position one: women should not be ordained

Some Christians believe that women should never be ordained because that's what the Bible teaches. They might state their position something like this:

For most of history, the church has not ordained women, neither on the Catholic nor the Protestant sides. The ordination of women is a recent notion that arose from the feminist movement. It is contrary to both Holy Scripture and church tradition. The apostle Paul was very clear when he said: "women should remain silent in the churches" (1 Cor. 14).

Men are the spiritual and administrative heads of their homes, and women should be submissive to them both at home and at church. When Paul said women should be quiet at church he meant exactly what he said: women should remain quiet at church! The Bible says it, and the Bible says it very clearly—women shouldn't speak in church.

If you wonder whether Paul really meant this or was writing only to a single church, look at the way he repeated this same command in 1 Timothy, chapter 2. Here Paul said it even more clearly. He told us exactly what his practice was: "I do not permit a woman to teach or have authority over a man; she must be silent."

What more do we need? Isn't that clear enough? Women should not have authority over men, and they should not be speaking at church. Period. Sure, it's OK for them to speak to children or to teach each other, but they cannot teach or lead men. Thus, a woman can't be an ordained preacher, a position of authority that requires them to teach and preach to men. The Bible is very clear on this issue, and that should be enough for us.

position two: women should be ordained

Other Christians, including the author of this book, believe that women may be ordained and that the ordination of women not only does not violate biblical teaching but actually is supported by Scripture. Their argument can be stated like this:

While Paul does appear to restrict women from speaking in church in two specific places in Scripture, he did so because of the social environment of that day. He was not making a rule for all time. Like his admonition that slaves should obey their masters, this rule was intended to be advice on how Christians should get along in the first century. It was never meant to be a universal rule, applied to all Christians, everywhere, all the time.

There have always been women who were active in God's service, even though women were considered second class citizens in ancient days. At Pentecost, Peter claimed that the Old Testament prediction that sons *and daughters* would prophecy had been fulfilled (Acts 2:16–17). We don't know their names, but certainly this prophecy was being lived out by some women in the early church. In fact, Philip had four daughters who prophesied (Acts 21:9). Prophecy was the first century equivalent of preaching.

does God call women to the ministry? if He does, then He certainly must expect them to serve

Besides, if Paul was so opposed to women being leaders, what would we conclude about Priscilla, an obvious tower of power in the book of Acts? Or, how about Phoebe (Rom. 16:1–2), whom Paul calls a *minister* from Cenchrea? At the close of the book of Romans, he commends "Junia, outstanding among the *apostles*" (16:7). It wasn't until the middle ages that the translators of the Bible changed the female name *Junia* to the male name *Junias*. And what about Paul's statement in Galatians that "In Christ . . . there is neither slave nor free, male and female" (3:28)? Did he mean that or not?

Yet even on top of all this evidence, there is an even more important argument. Consider the *trajectory of Scripture* (or the *heaven trajectory*). Is there any doubt that God intends for women and men to be fully equal in heaven? Shouldn't we be trying to move toward heaven instead of basing our model for the church on the fall of humanity?

But the most important question in this debate is this: Does God call women to the ministry? If He does, then He certainly must expect them to serve. The resistance against women in the ministry will be temporary, like the resistance to the abolition of slavery, which also made use of several proof texts. Eventually, women will have full access to the ministry; it will just take time. Not even a hundred years have passed since women gained the right to vote! In 1920 the United

States granted voting rights to women, and as recently as 1971 Switzerland—a real holdout on the issue—finally gave in. It's no wonder that the church is also coming around slowly on the ordination of women. Social change takes time. Someday women will be ordained in all denominations, including the Roman Catholic Church.

Until then, women will find a place of service. If God calls an Asian, or a Black, or a single person, or a white person, He always has a place of service in mind for them. If you are a woman and God calls you, He will provide a place for you to serve, too. Your denomination may refuse to ordain you, but some denomination will do it. No one denomination is strong enough to keep you out of the ministry if God has called you into it. The Roman Catholic Church was once so universal and powerful (during the Middle Ages) that they could block all women from ordination, but not today. A woman called to the ministry today will find a place of service—either in her own denomination or in mine.

challenges for women in the ministry

This book is not neutral on this issue. It promotes the ordination of women. When women are ordained, however, they face some special challenges. If you are a woman who has been called to the ministry, you must obey. But be forewarned: life as a minister may be much harder for you than for your male counterparts. That's not a pleasant fact, but it's true,

> if you are a woman and God calls you, He will provide a place for you to serve, too

at least for now. And since it is true, you knowing so from the start will help you prepare for your life in the ministry.

finding a job

One of the primary problems for women in the ministry is finding a job. Most denominations aren't interested in maintaining a gender balance among either employees or leaders. Most churches (particularly in America) let "the people" have a voice in the selection of their pastor. There are a few exceptions, of course. Some churches have an Episcopal form of government and place ministers in churches without much involvement by the local members. But since most denominations let congregations have a say in selecting their pastor, a church can have a *preference* for some types of pastors over others, just as voters do in political elections. The line between preference and prejudice, of course, is razor thin.

> if a denomination permits local people to interview prospective ministers and vote on their selection, both personal and congregational preferences will affect the outcome

When a congregation is deciding who will be its new pastor, especially a new senior pastor or preacher, it usually examines several résumés. The church members will examine your training, gifts, skills, along with your references. They'll look at your church involvement in college and seminary and your track record at other churches. But they'll consider other things too, even if they don't admit it out loud. For instance, many churches will prefer a married minister over a single man or woman. Many will prefer a couple with children over a couple with no children. Lots of churches will prefer a pastor with a young family over an older minister who is an empty-nester. A single man with no female interests whatsoever has a very difficult time getting a ministry job. And many local churches will "prefer" a man over a woman as their minister. That's true not just of male members but female members too.

All this sounds very unfair, and it is. But if a denomination permits local people to interview prospective ministers and vote on their selection, both personal and congregational preferences will affect the outcome. These preferences—and prejudices—will be determined far more by hundreds of years of sociology than by sound theology or biblical exegesis.

It may be unfair, even outright wrong, but it is true. If you are a woman entering the ministry, you need to recognize this now. Indeed, if you are a single man, or black, Asian, overweight, have gray hair, or have no children, you should recognize this factor as well. A local church's preferences and prejudices will affect your hiring even after you've "made the cut" based on your competence and accomplishments.

For these churches, selecting a minister is something like selecting a spouse. College students don't try to be fair or give everyone an equal chance when deciding whom to date. Usually, they prefer to spend time with the people they like, and they don't even consider dating people who are unattractive just to "be fair" to them. Churches who tip the scale on otherwise equal candidates based on personal preferences think of themselves as doing the same thing as you might do when looking for a date. (They aren't doing that, but that's what they *think*.) Most of these churches don't believe they are doing anything wrong, assuming that they are even conscious of doing it in the first place.

So, if you are a woman going into the ministry, you may have to be more qualified than the men who interview for the same position. Luckily, that's not difficult. Women tend to have some traits that make them better equipped for some elements of the ministry. Perhaps that is why God calls both women and men into the ministry. Men and women both have traits that the ministry needs. Just as God wants both men and women to take part in raising children in the home, so He also seems to want both men and women to use their dominant strengths to raise strong spiritual children in the church.

resistance to your ministry

But getting a job is not the only extra challenge you will face as a woman minister. Even after you get a job, there may be people in your church who resist your ministry, especially your preaching. It may surprise you to discover that the deepest resistance will come not from men but from other women. If you get sick and have to miss a Sunday in the pulpit, they'll crack jokes about you being "the weaker sex." If you decide to stay home and care for your preschool daughter when she has an ear infection, some unkind people will remark, "She's doing the mommy thing." And if you decide to stay at home for an entire decade in order to raise your children as a stay-at-home mom, some will wonder what happened to your call and question your lifetime ordination. They'll even try to use you as an example when dismissing the ordination of women altogether.

> if you are a woman going into the ministry, you may have to be more qualified than the men who interview for the same position

If you are in a denomination where there are few women in the ministry, you'll get invited to the meetings for minister's wives, and when you attend mostly-male ministerial retreats, you may have trouble finding a ride with a fellow minister unless there is a group going together. If you are a co-minister with your husband, it will be easier. But if you have a husband outside of the ministry, people won't exactly know how to deal with him as a pastor's *husband*. When you invite people to your parsonage, you'll have to sort out who is the social entertainer and who will do the cooking. And there will be a hundred other little things that you'll notice about being a woman in ministry that seem to make it harder for you.

But what can you do? If you are called to the ministry, can you walk away from it? If you are truly called, can you decide that it's not worth it? Thus the real question for all men and women headed for the ministry, but especially for women, is "Am I really called?" In fact, the answer to that question may be your only defense against people who oppose your being in the pulpit. To debate this topic based on various Bible texts usually just gets you into a dart tossing contest. Let's face it, both the people who promote the ordination of women and those who oppose it use the same Bible. That is not to say that the Bile is unclear on these points, just that we have not found a churchwide consensus on this yet. Until we do, it may be that the best thing you can say to defend your ordination against critics is "God called me."

If you are truly called, then you must find a place of ministry. This is not to say that you shouldn't try to change the thinking of your denomination and the people in it—you should. But being an activist for change on this issue will probably not be your primary calling. Your calling will be the same that as that of most men who are called to the ministry: to be a prophet and priest for the people of God, to represent God to the people, and the people to God. Indeed, more men should be leading the charge on bringing change in this area.

finding a place to serve

If you are a called woman, God has a place of service for you. God wasn't playing games when He called you. You might have to change denominations—as hard as that would be—but you *will* find a place to exercise your gifts. Remember, God is far less concerned about what label you wear than about you being an equipping minister to His universal church. God is not a Baptist, Nazarene, Methodist, Presbyterian, or Wesleyan. He is the Lord of the Church Universal. God's call to you was never a denominational call anyway. It was a call to be a minister in the church universal. In fact, many denominations recognize that fact by commissioning ministers to serve both their own flock "and the church universal." So if you are called by God to His universal church and your denomination refuses to confirm that call by ordaining you, what else can you do? You must find a denomination that does accept women in the ministry and join them. God won't be disappointed. This sounds drastic, and many women would rather "stay and fight" than leave the denomination they love. Fighting for this cause, however, can take a toll. Despair and bitterness are wounds this battle sometimes inflicts. As a young woman, search your heart carefully on this matter. If your denomination is turning back the clock by refusing to ordain women, you may have to jump ship in order to save your ministry.

Face it, some denominations have never ordained women and they don't intend to start. Unfortunately, some major evangelical denominations have recently turned back the clock and discontinued the ordination of women, even ousting from the ministry those women who were already ordained. Shame on those denominations! But there are lots of denominations that welcome both men and women into the ministry, and these denominations will increasingly become the place of service for women who are called into God's work. Some of these churches will actually encourage your calling and provide ready opportunities for you. Most, however, will just give you a chance to "make the church grow." Most will not give you any preferential treatment, and they'll expect you to produce a good track record. But they will give you a chance, and they *will* ordain you.

> there are lots of denominations that welcome both men and women into the ministry, and these denominations, will increasingly become the place of service for women who are called into God's work

When they do, use your gifts and graces to produce the fruit of ministry wherever you go. Prove that you can minister to a congregation and reach out to the unchurched. Do your best to make the church grow. For even people who are highly prejudiced on this issue are usually impressed with fruit. And district and denominational leaders *always* are! People may tell you that women shouldn't go fishing, but if you catch a string of giant fish for the Kingdom, don't worry, they won't tell you to toss them back! Producing the fruit in your ministry will guarantee you greater freedom in the future.

So know this: if you are a woman headed for the ministry, it may be hard, but if you are truly called, you must obey. God doesn't call people as a trick; He won't call you if He has no place for you to serve. If He's called you, go for it. If you can't do that in your own church, switch to a more female-friendly denomination. But whatever you do, do not abandon your calling just because it is difficult. Certainly you could at least (at least?!) plant a church, like the Apostle Paul did.

The apostles in Jerusalem didn't give Paul a church; in fact, they encouraged him to go home to Tarsus and get out of their hair. So what did he do? He went out and started his own string of churches. He raised his own support and eventually wound up sending financial aid back to the very people who had told him to go home. Who would stop you from planting a church? And if you did, guess who would attend? You'd reach people who are completely open to a woman minister. If they weren't, they wouldn't come in the first place. Your gender wouldn't even be an issue! So if you are called by God, there is a ministry for you. Where there's a call, there's a way.

where to go from here

So are you a woman called to the ministry? What should you do about it? First, clarify your call so that it becomes a burning certainty. You'll need that certainty in the ministry. Second, be encouraged that in spite of the first two thousand years of church history, women like you have made great progress in the last century. Third, know that someday the church of the future will be shocked that there was a time when some churches refused to ordain women, and they'll remember you as a pioneer. Fourth, find a good woman minister as a mentor to help you develop the savvy you'll need to "work the system" in your future ministry. Finally, be encouraged. God values you, or He wouldn't have called you. God can be trusted. He does not call up workers if He has no job for them.

exploring your call

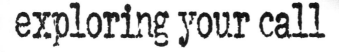

to share

1. Tell about a woman minister you have met or heard speak. Describe her ministry.
2. Tell about your own personal preferences and prejudices for whom you would want to be your pastor. Include prejudices other than male versus female, and be honest. Don't condemn others without confessing yourself.

to discuss

1. How does a denomination go about changing its traditions? That is, how would a denomination come to adopt a different stand on ordaining women?
2. This book argues that a call must be confirmed by the church. What should a person do if no church anywhere will ordain him or her, and even their attempts to start an independent church never get off the ground? What advice would you give to such a person?
3. There are many in-between positions on this issue. For instance, some argue for (married) women to be submissive at home but equal at church. Others argue that a woman may be ordained but only for staff work, never to serve as a senior pastor or preacher. Without committing yourself too quickly on these issues, explore them in discussion with others.

to do

1. Using all the Scriptures listed in this chapter, make a chart that shows how you are inclined to interpret them. Find someone who disagrees with you to help you refine it.
2. Interview a woman who is in ordained ministry and hear her story. If

none are available, interview a woman who is called to the ministry and get her take on this issue and the obstacles she thinks she will face or has already faced.

8

How has God been preparing me for the ministry? Does it start when I sense the call or did it begin the moment I was born, maybe even before? How can God use everything that happens to me—both good and bad—to make me a more effective minister? What is the program God uses to develop a minister?

God's fingerprints on your life

You have been in ministerial training for a long time. While it might seem as if God simply decided to call you into the ministry one day, He has known about your call for a long time. And all this time He has been preparing you. He has been preparing you by:

- Granting you spiritual gifts to use in His work.
- Stirring up passion in your heart for certain causes.
- Helping you develop personal abilities to use in the ministry.
- Molding your personality to suit your future ministry.

- Permitting all kinds of experiences in your life—both good and bad—from which you could develop wisdom.

- Bringing people, events, spiritual experiences, and even organizations into your life to develop your ministerial potential.

God has even been using negative events to prepare you for your ministry. For instance, you might see a bad experience as a terrible blot in your life—your parents' divorce, for example. God is always taking bad stuff and making a treasure out of it. God may have seen your parents' divorce as an opportunity for you to develop sensitivities that you'll need to help people in the future. Or He may have used an experience like that to shape the attitude about marriage that you'll need in order to minister to others. Consider this story:

My dad left my mother when I was fourteen. To tell the truth, he cheated on my mom and got caught. They had never gotten along very well, and he was gone most evenings anyway. He was absent during almost all of the important moments of my life, and he occasionally came home drunk, and sometimes even hit my mom. Even though he was not a very good dad, I still loved him, and when he finally left us I felt abandoned. To be honest, it still hurts now as I write about it.

But now I can see that God was teaching me, even through this painful experience. For instance, I'm very sensitive to anything I might do that would hurt others the way I've been hurt. It hasn't made me hard or bitter, but softer toward other people. And another thing: I decided to never start drinking, and I never did, even in high school. I am also very cautious about whom I might marry, because I believe this: once we are married it will be for life, no matter what. I will never leave my wife or abandon my own children the way my dad did me. I will also be far more sensitive to the pain of teens in my church whose parents are getting a divorce. I think I'll be able to minister more effectively to them. As painful as it all was, I honestly think I can be a better minister to others because of the lessons I've learned.

This is an example of God's program for developing a minister. He uses life experiences—both good and bad—to train us for ministry to others. It's not that He *causes* bad things to happen. God doesn't cause fathers to abandon their children just to teach a lesson! But even though the things people do may be wrong, God can still use the resulting experience for good. Joseph's brothers did an evil deed when they sold him into slavery, but "God meant it for good."

If you are called to the ministry it would be a wonderful project for you to reflect on the experiences of your life—your gifts, abilities, personality, and passions—to see if you can discern how God has been preparing you. Rick Warren, pastor of Saddleback church in Orange Country, California, has popularized a way of thinking about one's life based on the acronym S.H.A.P.E. That represents

> God uses life experiences—both good and bad—to train us for ministry to others

Spiritual gifts, Heart (passion), Abilities, Personality, and Experiences. Thinking about those categories will help anyone look at the past to discover how God has been molding him or her for the future. That exercise is especially helpful for a future minister. For in looking back, you will find plenty of God's "fingerprints" on your life. As you read this chapter, reflect on your own life and see if you can detect evidence that God was at work—perhaps even before you were born.

spiritual gifts

God does not give spiritual gifts to individuals so much as He gives those gifts to His church *through* the individual (see 1 Cor. 12:7; Eph. 4:11, Rom. 12:3–8). The gifts are not for you but for His church. They are to be used by you for the benefit of others. This can be confusing because we in the church sometimes ask "What is *your* spiritual gift?" as if the gift is owned by the individual. The gifts are given to God's church, but you and I carry these gifts as stewards. So what does the church need? It needs people to serve, using the gifts that have been entrusted to them. The church needs people with wisdom. It needs people with hospitality. The church needs people with gifts of leadership, music, or prayer. The church needs people with great faith, the ability to administer, to teach, to counsel, to discern, and a dozen other gifts.

Individuals do not need these gifts so much as the church needs them, the body of Christ. Thus God grants to Christians certain supernatural abilities in order that they may build up the church, equipping others to do God's work on earth.

Which spiritual gift might you have? There are several lists in the Bible (1 Cor. 12; Eph. 4; Rom. 12); however, many scholars believe these lists are not intended to be exhaustive but are merely examples of the many gifts that God gives. The church needs spiritual gifts today, such as musical ability or leading worship, that are implied but not explicitly stated in these three lists. In fact, some say that taking a test to discover your spiritual gifts can actually confuse a young minister since the test only measures what the person sees in him- or herself, not what others perceive about him or her. Then too, since the church is the primary recipient of the gift, some gifts may emerge over time or in certain congregations as a minister moves through life. Nevertheless, spiritual gifts tests have been popular since the 1960s and may help you begin the search for your own gifts.

You can begin to develop an understanding of your spiritual gifts by asking this question: What supernatural abilities does God seem to be growing in me *to help His church?* Make a preliminary list of these things, and you might catch an early glimpse of what God is giving the church through you. Start with the gifts mentioned in the Scriptures listed above, or just start by listing the gifts others have observed in you.

what supernatural abilities does God seem to be growing in me *to help His church?*

Since every Christian has some spiritual gift or gifts, we might ask how this subject relates to the professional ministry to which you are called. Here's how: your gift will greatly affect the way in which you do ministry. For instance, if you have a great gift of showing mercy, the church or youth group you lead will likely be shaped around that gift, simply because you are the group's leader. In fact, this is a point of caution for those entering the ministry: we sometimes try to create a church in the image of our own gifts rather than allowing the church to reflect all the gifts God has given to it.

But there is an even more important issue for those called to the ministry. There are some spiritual gifts especially oriented toward equipping ministry. While you may not see them emerging yet (especially if you have not had the opportunity to use them), most men and women called to the ministry sooner or later exhibit gifts in preaching, teaching, pastoring, leadership, and caring.

So what spiritual gifts do you see emerging in your life? What is God giving the church through you?

heart or passion

What do you get excited about? What makes you angry? Are you especially burdened about something that others don't seem to care about? What really gets you cranked up or makes your heart leap? These are the *passions* of your heart. Old saints used to call these *burdens*. They believed that God laid particular burdens on certain individuals, and those people were supposed to major on that cause or ministry. They were right.

For instance what *people group* do you seem to care about more than others? Teens? Minorities? College students? People in the military? The poor? The sick? Parents? People in foreign lands? Older folk?

Or, what *issues* stir up your heart and even make you angry? Does your heart break for those suffering from poverty? Drugs? Abortion? Child abuse? Ignorance? Lack of adequate housing? Materialism? War? Injustice? Often, the issues you care about the most correlate with the people group for which you are most burdened.

Your spiritual gift comes from God and is for use primarily in building up the church (though sometimes it is used in the world too, of course). This is also true of your passion, particularly if you are called to the ministry. Those who are not called to work with the church often fulfill their passion in their career, but for ministers, this passion is usually worked out inside the church, though not always. As far as the church goes, it works like this: God lays various burdens upon different individuals so that, all together, they will keep the church balanced. While nobody else at the church may seem to care much about one person's "pet issue," God often calls these individuals to remind the church of the total scope of the mission. These folk will "harp on it" until others join the cause or at least recognize that the cause is a legitimate part of the church's work.

Remember though, God doesn't give you a passion just so that you can tell the church what to do. It is primarily to tell *you* what to do. If you have a personal burden for poor people who cannot afford decent housing, God may want you to be a prophet, reminding your church that they should support groups like Habitat for Humanity. Your burden, however, is not simply a burden to nag others. It is a personal burden for *you* to make that ministry a major part of your own service: building houses, serving on boards, raising funds. In fact, when you do that you will be an agent of the church. The church often does its work by sending one or two persons. The whole army does not need to go out on every mission. God lays burdens on the hearts of individuals so that the church will be balanced, each part doing its own work.

> an ability or skill is a natural or developed gift, something you were born with or developed through training and experience

So what does all this talk about passion and heart have to do with your ministry? *Every* Christian should have some God-given passion of the heart, not just ministers. A minister must determine if his or her burdens are merely the personal passions of a private Christian or are God-given burdens that should be passed on to the entire church. As with spiritual gifts, a minister may be tempted to recreate the church in the image of his or her own burdens. Sometimes this is what God wants, and that may be why God places you in a particular church at a particular time. But at other times, God gives the minister a personal passion and the minister must work as an individual Christian to fulfill the work at hand and not expect the entire church to take up the same cause. It will take great discernment for you to sort out which of your God-given passions are meant for you personally and which are meant to be shared with the entire church.

Do you sense any personal burdens or passions that you think are from God? Is God laying a certain group of people on your heart now? What issues are burning within you? What passions are emerging?

abilities and skills

At first glance your abilities and skills may seem a lot like your spiritual gifts. In fact, one's abilities and spiritual gifts do overlap, but there is a difference. Abilities are natural or developed aptitudes and are not directly God-given. A spiritual gift is a supernatural gift, a God-given ability that is primarily directed toward the church. An ability or skill is a natural or developed gift, something you were born with or developed through training and experience. But of course, all these so-called natural abilities are also from God, since He created us, so the difference can be difficult to discern.

Let's say you have wonderful skill at playing basketball. It seems like you were born with it, though you've developed and honed it along the way. It is not a spiritual gift with which you are supposed to use to build up the church so much as it is a natural ability. Or perhaps you are really talented at woodworking. You can make a handmade clock that looks perfect. Or maybe you are good at fixing mechanical things. Perhaps you are a great cook and like to fix fancy meals. Maybe you have a wonderful eye for graphics and can immediately see how things fit together on a page or instantly sense "what goes with what" in decorating a house. All these are probably natural abilities more than spiritual gifts. That does not mean they are of no spiritual value. All good things are from God and should be used to glorify Him. But we might say that these abilities come indirectly from God and are hints at what your contribution to God's world mission might be.

So what does this have to do with the ministry? Many ministers have similar abilities and skills. While there is no test that will tell you for sure that God has called you to the ministry, there are some excellent tests that will measure your abilities, personality, and skills. Taking these tests will tell how you match up with other ministers. For instance, the ability to get along with people is a commonly held skill among ministers. If you don't have this skill, you'll have to develop it. And most ministers have developed the skill of leading others (they may also have the spiritual gift of leadership). Most ministers have gained, either naturally or supernaturally, the ability to do public speaking, since presenting the gospel or teaching others is a primary part of their calling. These abilities can be spiritual gifts, natural abilities, or both.

But don't get the idea that having an ability always means you will enjoy doing it. Many ministers have great ability for public speaking, but not all ministers enjoy it. Some ministers get sick every week before they preach, and some have a headache for twelve hours after! But they do a great job while preaching. When people hear them, they assume it must be easy for them to do and that they love it. Our calling does not always make us comfortable, but if we are obedient we can be effective. God has not called us to His work to make us happy. He has called us to be effective in accomplishing His will on earth: bringing in the kingdom of God.

On the other hand, don't expect to hate what you are doing. God does not call us to be miserable but obedient. Almost all ministers *enjoy* doing what they are called to do. Just don't expect that everything you do will make you feel happy. You might dread preaching yet still win hundreds to Christ and cause thousands to grow spiritually through your life. Your abilities are hints from God of how He might use you in the future.

So, what abilities do you seem to have? Don't be afraid to list things that do not seem spiritual. List them all. What are your skills? What are you good at? What do these hints tell you about the kind of ministry God may be preparing for you?

personality and style

Do you like to be with people or would you rather work alone on a computer? Are you a hard-driving leader or more laid-back? Are you a take-charge leader or do you prefer to make decisions by consensus? Do you talk a lot when you are in a group or are you quiet, even shy? Do you like big groups of acquaintances or would you rather be with a small cell of really close friends? Do people see you as happy or as somber? Funny, thoughtful, or both? These questions are all matters of your personality and style. They reveal the person that you are, or at least the person you come across as being.

God can either change your personality or give you the strength to do what doesn't seem natural to you

There is no one personality type that God calls into His ministry. God calls outgoing people like the Apostle Peter, but he also calls introverted, melancholy types like Moses. Sure, most ministers appear to be outgoing. They have to be in order to work with people. But many are really shy people who simply demand of themselves a more outgoing style because the ministry needs it.

Thus it is dangerous to assume that you are not called to the ministry because you are "not like most ministers." God knows what He is doing, and calls whomever He wants for His ministry. If you are naturally shy, somewhat introverted, don't like parties, and are afraid to speak in front of large groups (like the author of this book) yet God calls you, He will provide the grace for you to do what He has called you to do. God can either change your personality or give you the strength to do what doesn't seem natural to you. You can do it because you love God and His people, and it accomplishes His will, even though you may feel unnatural when doing it.

One more thing. Don't be too quick to label yourself or accept labels others try to stick on you. People change. You will too. The way others see you may not be the way you really are. And even if it is, sometimes the "real you" can change. Many ministers at age thirty are quite different than they were at age nineteen. If they had made irreversible decisions about their future at a young age, they would have wound up somewhere far from the place of service God eventually led them to. God can change us, and we

> if God has been preparing you for the ministry all along, you will see evidence of that in what you've faced up to now, both good and bad

can even change ourselves. So we are not stuck with being exactly like we are today. So if God calls you, no matter what your personality, respond, and trust His grace to make you what He wants you to be.

So what kind of personality and style do you have so far? What traits seem to be emerging? What sort of a minister will you probably be as you start out? Where have you seen changes in your personality already? What future changes do you hope to see so that you can become an effective minister?

experiences and history

This chapter began with the statement that God's program for making a minister involves using life experiences to develop that person and teach wisdom. So far, this chapter has dealt mostly with the things that characterize you right now: your spiritual gifts, natural abilities and skills, and personality.

Now we look back to the things that have influenced you since birth—and even before. If God has been preparing you for the ministry all along, you will see evidence of that in what you've faced up to now, both good and bad. God's fingerprints are all over your life right now, but they are all over your past too. What was God trying to teach you in each experience or through each person you've encountered? As you look for God's fingerprints on your life, you might consider these five categories of experience.

people

Who are the people in your past whom God may have used to teach you about life and ministry? Think not just about the good experiences with people but also about the bad examples and influences. Sometimes the lessons we learn from bad models can be even more powerful than those from good models! Who in your family did God use to teach and train you? What was He trying to teach through each person? What teachers had a great influence on you, and what might God have been teaching you through them? What have you learned through your friends? Enemies? If you made a list of all the people in your life who had an impact on you, what would you list as the life and ministry lessons from each person?

You might not be able to guess exactly what God had in mind with each experience, but you can try. When you've reflected on your entire life in this way, you will see God's fingerprints emerging. Before you ever imagine that God would call you to the ministry, He sent people to cross your path who would teach and train you.

events

So much for people, what about events? What events in your life, both good and bad, have had the greatest influence on you so far? Think about family experiences, crisis events, and important moves. Consider negative experiences like an auto wreck, a divorce, or the death of a loved one. What might God have wanted you to learn through these event? What principles? What wisdom? What commitments for your own life and ministry? What are the major events of your life, and how did God plan to use them to mold you for the ministry?

spiritual experience

What was the first spiritual experience you remember? Were you a child? A teen? When did you become a Christian? Have you made fresh commitments to God since then? Did God ever come to you in a personal spiritual experience that was life changing? Did you have some sort of spiritual experience when you were called to the ministry? Was there a retreat, camp, or worship experience where God moved powerfully in your life? If you made a list or chart of all these spiritual experiences in chronological order, what pattern would emerge? What do you think God has been trying to accomplish in you through these experiences? What was He teaching you that will help you minister to others?

leadership experience

Have you ever been in charge of anything? Did you ever organize a club or a sleepover when you were a kid? Did you have a job where you were given some leadership responsibility? Have you ever taught a Sunday school class or helped with the youth group? Did you ever have a leadership role in student government, sports, or music? Think of all the roles you've had—in the family, at school, in the neighborhood, at church, and elsewhere. Have you ever influenced others in these roles? If you listed your previous leadership responsibilities and reflected on them, what pattern would form? How might God have been at work training you for future leadership through these experiences?

organizations and institutions

Finally, what organizations and institutions are dominant in your life? What local churches have you been a part of? What denominations? Were you involved with a ministry like Fellowship of Christian Athletes or Young Life during high school? What schools have you attended? What conferences or conventions did you go to? Were you in the Scouts? What other clubs, organizations, or institutions have influenced you? If you listed them all and reflected on the list, what would emerge as you connected the dots? What was God up to when He permitted you to interact with these organizations and institutions? Can you see His fingerprints?

God did not start preparing you for the ministry at the moment you were called. He has been preparing you ever since you were born, even before. Your past has God's fingerprints all over it. Unfortunately, most people never take the time to write out the lists mentioned above. Since they never list the dots—the moments when God was at work in their lives—they can never connect them and see the pattern. While they vaguely recognize that God has been at work in the past, they never take the time to reflect specifically on those experiences, and they do not see the shape of things to come.

Past experiences are often secret clues to future ministry. So why not stop reading this book right now, and start making the lists mentioned in this chapter. You might see more of God's fingerprints in your past than you ever imagined, and it might be a good break from reading this book!

exploring your call

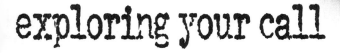

to share

1. Tell about one very positive person in your past and what God may have been teaching you through that person.
2. Share one negative experience from your past and suggest how God may be trying to use that experience for good, both right now and to shape your future ministry.

to discuss

1. What is the difference between God *causing* and *using* a negative experience in your life? Or, if you are a particularly deep thinker, try this one: If God could have prevented some negative thing in your life but chose not to, is He then ultimately responsible for everything that has happened to you, even the bad things?
2. If you want to think about hard things, then try discussing this: Does God call people as He needs them, or does God know whom He is planning to call even before they are born? Exercise your theological mind on this one: How would you prove your position either way? How would it change your view of God or the way we relate to Him? When you've finished the discussion, switch to the subject of prayer. Decide how this same principle would apply to our prayers.

to do

1. Interview a minister over lunch or for about an hour. Ask questions based on this chapter in order to construct a *life map* of his or her gifts, abilities, personality, people, events, etc., that God used in developing that person for the ministry. Speak with someone who has enough ministry experience to comment on how early experiences were used in later ministry and how some experiences became less important over time.

2. Jump in with both feet and try to make your own life map, including all the charts listed in this chapter. Look for clues from your past that point toward what God is planning for your future. Aim to discover who you are becoming and discern your own trajectory.

9

What sort of jobs are there for an ordained minister? Does everyone have to be a senior pastor, or are there other jobs to do in the church? What are the most common ministry jobs available to graduates? What other staff jobs are there besides youth pastor? Are all ministry jobs in the local church? What about parachurch ministries?

kinds of
ministry jobs

entering the ministry as your life's vocation does not mean you are limited forever to being a youth pastor, or that the only job available to you is being the preacher at a country crossroads church. This chapter describes all kinds of jobs that an ordained minister might fill during his or her ministry. In fact, many ministers have filled several of these jobs by the time they are forty or so years old. So the question this chapter answers is "What kind of jobs are available for an ordained minister?"

jobs for ordained ministers

There are generally two classifications of church workers: *ordained ministers* and *lay workers*. Ordained ministers are called by God and confirmed by the church; they are set apart as the church's spiritual and administrative leaders. There are some jobs in the church that are reserved for ordained ministers while other jobs might be filled by either an ordained minister or a lay staff worker. The vast majority of church ministry jobs are held by ordained ministers, but we shall see that there are also some jobs in church work for nonordained people.[1]

solo pastor

By far the most common job for a minister is solo pastor, someone who works without any pastoral staff members in a small or average-sized church. The vast majority of churches in North America have a staff of one—the pastor. In fact, in most denominations the vast majority of churches average seventy-five people or fewer. A church of that size can seldom afford two ministers. So in most churches, the music minister, the worship pastor, the youth pastor, and the children's minister are all one person: the solo pastor. In a church this size the pastor's "staff" is composed of volunteers, laypeople who attend the church.

> though many ministers start out in staff positions, most eventually come to lead their own congregations

If you're used to attending a larger church, the idea of being a solo pastor might be unimaginable to you now. Perhaps your own model of a minister is a youth pastor or worship minister, and you've seen the preaching pastor as someone far older and more mature than you ever plan to be. (Sorry, you'll actually be that old someday!) Though many ministers start out in staff positions, most eventually come to lead their own congregations. You may not imagine being the pastor of older, wiser folk until you are much older and wiser yourself, but if God leads you to do this, He will provide the wisdom, authority, and anointing for you to do the work. The solo pastor enjoys by far the greatest variety of work. Solo pastors get to do a little of all the work of

---

[1] The term *job* is used here to indicate the notion of employment—working and getting paid for it. Ministry, of course, is not so much a job as a calling, but for this chapter it may be easiest to speak of jobs or job openings in order to communicate the kinds of work that are available to an ordained minister.

ministry and don't have to focus their skills and attention as narrowly as most other ministers do.

youth pastor

Probably the second most common job among church vocations is youth pastor. Rare before the 1960s, most churches with more than seventy-five in attendance try to hire at least a part-time youth minister nowadays. An ordained youth pastor does all the things a solo or senior pastor does, only with students. The students in the youth group are the congregation, and the youth minister does all the regular pastoral tasks including preaching, leading, counseling, visiting, and even performing religious rituals like Holy Communion and weddings for graduates or collegians. Because youth ministry provides such broad experience, many youth ministers eventually move into solo or senior pastor roles when they get older. Many larger churches turn to their former youth pastors when recruiting a new senior pastor, ten years or so later.

staff minister

Youth pastors really are in this category, but since there are so many youth pastor jobs, it's helpful to think of them separately. Before 1960 there were relatively few megachurches (churches over 1,000 in average attendance); thus, almost all new ministers became solo pastors. Since the 1960s there has been a virtual explosion of medium-sized churches and megachurches. Churches of 300, 700, 1,000, or even 5,000 people have become much more common. These churches typically have large staffs of ministers to care for all those people. In fact, these larger churches generally hire one minister for about every seventy-five to one hundred people in the congregation. While a church of one hundred probably has one minister, a church of one thousand might have ten. As you can see, the pastor-to-people ratio is about the same.

The explosion of larger churches has provided scores of new jobs for ministers. For example, you might serve as a worship pastor and direct the worship services as an ordained minister. Or you might get a job as minister of outreach or missions, and your responsibility would be to develop programs that get the people to reach out. In a job like that, you'd be leading the missions effort of the local church, including fund raising and mission trips. Or you could be the minister of Christian education and lead the discipleship and teaching ministry of the church. Or you might be the minister of assimilation and organize a church-wide effort to absorb visitors into the life of the church. There are

staff jobs have proliferated and become increasingly specialized

dozens of other staff jobs, including minister of children, music, evangelism, connections, and young adults. Some large churches even have an executive pastor, who works under the senior pastor and supervises all the other ministers. Churches often combine two or more of these responsibilities into a single position.

Staff job titles change as the church sees new needs or as new trends emerge. Fifty years ago, when the powerful teen culture emerged, the church invented the job of youth pastor as a response. As worship has increased in importance over the last few decades, the position of worship minister has emerged from what was once simply a music minister. The same is true with minister of assimilation or minister of small groups, or all other specialty jobs. New jobs are invented as congregational needs change.

Culture affects this too. In the 1950s, much of the work of the church was done by stay-at-home women who served as volunteers, supervised by a solo pastor. As more and more women left home and entered full-time employment, churches more often came to employ full-time ministers to do the work once done by these lay volunteers. Staff jobs have proliferated and become increasingly specialized. A solo pastor equates roughly to a general practitioner or family doctor in the medical profession. A staff pastor would be something like a specialist, such as an ophthalmologist or a surgeon. Educational institutions have responded to the demand for specialized ministers by offering a variety of ministry majors aimed at training men and women for these specialized jobs.

If you are headed for a staff ministry, it is important to get specialized training. It is also important that you do not narrow your options too soon, however, for churches tend to collect together several areas of responsibility and lump them into one job description. In fact, churches that hire a youth pastor often assign to that person a broad range of duties that would be better reflected in the title Minister of Youth, Worship, Hospital Visitation, Substitute Preacher, and Part-Time Janitor. Go ahead and specialize, but stay open to other areas and get your general training too—you never know what your second job may require! It is usually only in very large churches that staff ministers get to say, "I only do one thing."

ministry outside a local church

Most ministry jobs are in a local church, but not all. Some ordained ministers serve in a local church for years then become a district superintendent or bishop, leading and supervising many churches and their ministers. A few ministers get experience in a local church then become professors in an educational institution where they concentrate on teaching and training new ministers. Most denominations elect some of their ministers to serve the entire denomination by working at their national or world headquarters. Some ministers are sent into itinerant evangelism and travel around speaking or leading worship. Some denominations will appoint an ordained minister to work with parachurch organizations like Young Life, Kingdom Building Ministries, the Navigators, or Campus Crusade for Christ. Some ordained ministers are sent as missionaries to plant churches or train ministers in other cultures. But these jobs beyond the local church are the minority of opportunities for ministers.

> the ministry exists in order to serve the church, and ministers can't just decide on their own what they'll do or where they'll go

While an ordained minister might be appointed by his or her denomination to serve in any of these ministries, don't assume that you can simply choose what ministry job you'd like to do and then instruct your denomination to appoint you to it. You might hear God's leading personally, but it must be confirmed by the church. You can't ordain yourself. *The church* sets men and women apart for the ministry. When you accept ordination, you are submitting to the will of the church. The church will send you where you are needed. This submission to the church cannot be overemphasized. Learn it soon. Ministers are not free agents in developing their careers. The ministry exists in order to serve the church, and ministers can't just decide on their own what they'll do or where they'll go any more than soldiers can station themselves. Various churches have different forms of government, but they all agree on this point: an ordained person is not free to do whatever he or she pleases and call it "ministry." While you will have far more personal freedom than you would have in a military career, you must still be submissive to your denomination. If you cannot make the commitment to serve where your denomination appoints you, you should delay your ordination until you are willing to make that choice or find a denomination to which you are willing to submit. In fact, in most ordination vows the new minister must promise to submit to the church in these matters.

Sometimes we get our hobbies mixed up with our calling. I did that for many years. I absolutely love backpacking. In fact, my dream in life has been to go backpacking full-time, every day of the year, and take others along. I have always wanted to own and operate a little backpacking store where I could sell high-quality gear and get to know other backpackers. This has been my personal dream since I was in the seventh grade.

But I eventually realized that backpacking was my *hobby*, not my *calling*. Until I realized that I tried all kinds of ways to turn my hobby into my calling. It's difficult to find a church that will hire you as the minister of backpacking. I tried that. I even tried to find a scheme to get some church to appoint me for "backpacking evangelism," where I'd raise support and go hiking full-time while witnessing to other hikers. That didn't work either. Eventually, I came to realize that my calling is to the ministry but I could keep my hobby of backpacking as just that—a hobby. It could be recreation and rest from my calling. Hiking became my *vacation*, not my *vocation*.[2]

---

[2]An interesting sidelight to this story is that after many years I wound up at Indiana Wesleyan University where I both train future ministers and teach backpacking and camping courses. I spend most summers backpacking with my students now. Eventually, God merged my hobby into my ministry—but it happened thirty-five years after I tried to do it on my own.

senior pastor

While the term *senior pastor* is sometimes used to describe a solo pastor, we'll use the term here to mean a local church pastor who supervises one or more staff ministers. It is unlikely that you will finish your training and immediately land a job where there are other ministers working for you. You may one day be a senior pastor, however. Many senior pastors were once staff pastors. Often, young people who enter the ministry as a lifetime vocation say, "I can never see myself as a senior pastor." But of course, we can seldom see what God may lead us to do later in life. Can you picture yourself as a grandmother or grandfather?

It is very common for youth pastors to say, "I am going to stay in youth ministry for the rest of my life." That is a nice thing to say. It shows that they are very much committed to youth work. But there are very few youth ministers who are in their fifties, and even fewer ministers will retire from youth work at age seventy. God continues to place His fingerprints on our life,

> most of us should be cautious about boxing God in by announcing what we never intend to do

and sometimes our earlier ministry experiences are equipping us for things in the future that we'd never dreamed of doing. Most of us should be cautious about boxing God in by announcing what we never intend to do. Who knows, someday He might lead you to be a senior pastor who will be responsible for a large staff of other ministers. If that were to happen, you can know this for sure: God will equip you for whatever He leads you to do.

jobs for lay staff members

So far we have described all kinds of jobs in the church for ordained ministers because this book is written primarily about ordained ministry. But you should know there are other jobs in the church that do not require ordination. It seems confusing at first because we tend to think of everyone who works for the church as a minister. So when a church hires a former junior high school teacher to work full-time with the youth, we might call this person the youth pastor. Technically that person would be a youth *director.* A youth *pastor* is a licensed or ordained person who does youth ministry. (A licensed minister is someone who is preparing for ordination and has provisional approval to act as a minister while completing his or her training.) A youth *director* is a layperson doing similar work.

It is possible to go into church work without being an ordained or licensed minister. We know that is true for a church secretary and janitor. They work at the church, receive a paycheck for it, and do it as service for God and others, but they are not working as ordained ministers. This is true of other jobs in the church as well, jobs that might be filled by either ordained ministers or lay employees. A *director* of Christian education would be a layperson while a *minister* of Christian education would be an ordained or licensed person. *Director* of worship would be a layperson while a *minister* of worship would be an ordained or licensed person.

Why is this important? This is important because you will need to discern whether God is calling you toward ordained or lay ministry. Some men and women enter church vocations but do not intend to spend their entire life in that work. They know from the beginning that they will never accept the full responsibility of an ordained minister, will not accept a regular preaching assignment, and do not seek to have significant authority in the church. They never want to preside over serving the Lord's Supper, and wouldn't perform weddings or funerals, even if asked. They may see church work as a temporary thing, perhaps intending to do it for a few years before moving into another line of work.

> ordained ministers have far greater responsibility and much more authority than lay church workers

Does that describe you? If so, don't be discouraged from going into church work; there are jobs in the church for you. But if this describes your view of your whole life, then think twice about pursuing the ordained ministry. This is not mere semantics. There is a significant difference between full-time church work and the ordained ministry. Ordained ministers have far greater responsibility and much more authority than lay church workers. They generally receive much more training, are accorded greater trust, are called upon to make the tough decisions. They are also amenable to their denomination to a greater degree, and must serve where appointed. They have greater privileges too, since they offer the sacraments, are more often sought out for counseling or wisdom, and are usually eligible for leadership positions that laypeople are not. While they may do similar work in any given local church, there really is a difference between ordained ministers and lay staff workers.

You will want to search your heart on this matter. If God has clearly called you to the ministry for life—wherever that may lead you—then pursuing ordination is what most experienced ministers would counsel you to do. However, if you intend to do church work only for a few year before pursuing another career, then most experienced ministers would tell you to find a ministry job in the church, but not pursue ordination.

exploring your call

to share

1. What passions or hobbies do you have that you might be tempted to merge with your ministry?
2. Make a list of all the staff members at any church you have attended, tell what particular job they had and whether they were ordained ministers or laypeople. Share this list with a friend.

to discuss

1. List some reasons a person might have for becoming either an ordained minister or a lay staff person in the church. Which church jobs are better for ordained ministers and which fit best with lay staff workers?
2. If the ratio of ministers to members is about the same in smaller churches as in larger ones, which size do you think is best for organizing the church worldwide? What are the advantages and disadvantages of large churches? Small churches? How many people does a church need to make it viable, in your opinion?

to do

1. Make a chart of all of the kinds of jobs available in the church with a title for each. Organize the chart in three columns: *Ministry Job, Title for an Ordained Minister* and *Title for a Lay Staff Worker.* Use your imagination to come up with as many different job functions as possible and as many titles that accurately describe the position for either an ordained minister or a layperson.
2. Make a list of questions about a church job, then interview someone who holds that job but is not ordained and is not planning to be ordained. Share your findings with others.

Have you ever been tempted to think, "I'm called by God and the church already recognizes it. I'm going into the ministry without any more training because God needs me there now!" Why wouldn't you do that? Isn't it be better to go into church work immediately after high school rather than waste time going to college or seminary? Why go to classes while others go to hell? Couldn't you win more people to Christ if you skipped the preparation time and got to work now?

preparing
for the ministry

t he call to the ministry is a call to prepare. God is not so desperate that He has no other ministers to do His work until you show up. He knew the exact number of ministers He'd need in the world today even before the foundation of the world was laid. He is never caught shorthanded. When God calls a man or woman to His ministry, He knows there will be a time of preparation. He called the Apostle Paul, and Paul spent three years preparing in the desert, even though he had already graduated from training as a Jewish leader. Even God's Son, Jesus, spent decades in silent preparation before His public ministry began. Certainly if Jesus, the Son of God, had to prepare for decades, you and I should spend some time preparing as well.

The preparation of a minister has three primary elements: developing *character*, gaining *education,* and acquiring practical *training.* All three can and should happen simultaneously to make you a better minister. As you read this chapter, think about how you are developing in each area.

character

The ministry is a life of dealing with the souls of women and men, thus the state of your own soul is highly relevant. We sometimes refer to this state of the soul as *character.* Your personality is important for the ministry since this determines how people see you. Your reputation is important also because it is the collective judgment people have about you. Character alone, however, is paramount, for this is who you really are.

comprehensive character

Character is what you are inside where nobody sees you. It includes all your inner motives and the attitudes nobody else knows about. Character is the sum of these inner values, attitudes, motivations, thoughts, and desires. It is the real you, the person God knows perfectly. You don't even know your own character as well as God does. After God and you, those close to you know your character best. People who only know you in a shallow way probably know only your personality or your reputation. They probably don't know your character. But God knows your character, and so do you.

> character includes all your inner motives and the attitudes nobody else knows about

character revealed by actions

Character is revealed by our words, thoughts, and deeds. Others can't always see your real character, but they can see some evidence of it. They see your honesty, responsibility, loyalty, kindness, and humility—or lack thereof. They see you make the hard decision to do right when it costs you something, and they pronounce you a person of good character or a person with integrity. Others can see the effects of your inner character, though not your hidden character itself. So while character is invisible, the fruit of character is quite evident.

So why is character important to one called into the ministry? Because who you eventually become is a result of your character. Your inner character eventually produces outside behavior. When someone is caught in a lie or cheating on his or her spouse, we often focus most on the behavior: what they *did* that was wrong. But more important than the act is the source of the act: the weak, inner character. It is your character that keeps you from cheating on a test when nobody would ever find out. It is your character that enables you to get up and go to church when you feel like sleeping in. Character prompts you to pick up a piece of trash off the ground when no one is watching.

> we develop character through thousands of little decisions made a dozen times each day

It is character than enables you to say no when the culture and all your fleshly desires say yes. Character is secret, but its effects sooner or later are revealed as behavior and become evident to all.

strengthening character

Christian character can be developed. We are not born with Christian character; in fact, we are born sinful. We must develop character. How? First, by the action of the Holy Spirit. When we become Christians, the Holy Spirit enters us and makes an inner change. We have new desires, motivations, and strength of will. We have a strengthened character. This change at conversion, however, is not the end of the story. While our character is renewed, it still is weak at times.

So how does weak character get strong? God builds character. He starts building our character when we are saved and continues throughout life. But God does not do this without our cooperation. We cannot simply lie in bed every Sunday morning waiting for God to build in the character to get up and go to church! God works with us to build character. He teaches us what is right and then prompts us to do it. We then must then respond to Him by making the right choices (for example, setting an alarm so we can get up and go to church).

Thus, we develop character through thousands of little decisions made a dozen times each day. Each time I make a decision to do right, my character is strengthened. Each time I decide to do wrong, it weakens. As I continually choose to do the right thing, week after week, my character becomes a powerful spiritual muscle. My will becomes set, and what was once difficult becomes a normal habit of life. Exercise of the will builds "character muscles." Developing character takes regular workouts and repeated effort.

And we are not left alone to do this. God has given us the Holy Spirit as a personal trainer. He will guide you individually and personally, but more so, the Holy Spirit will use the church—the body of Christ—as a tool. One seldom develops character as a lone ranger. The church helps us develop character.

Since your character will determine your destiny, developing inner character is a primary task of ministry preparation. A few of the classes that you take for educational preparation may touch on character development, but your character will really be shaped by all of the things you do—not just the things you do in class. Martin Luther once remarked that the best preparation for a preacher was temptation. Why would he say that? Because temptation provides a chance to develop character by saying no. Each time we say no we develop the strength of will to say it again, and eventually, saying no to that particular temptation will become habitual. That's how we develop character.

You can develop some character completely on your own, but it is better to develop it with other people. This is where the church comes in, with accountability groups, mentoring, and spiritual direction, all to help us develop character. Connecting with others on your journey to develop sturdy Christian character will make the journey easier. A mentor, accountability partner, or spiritual director can help you establish the thousand strands of thread that will become a heavy rope of integrity, your character.

Thus, a mind shift is needed for many men and women preparing for the ministry. As a minister in training, you must understand this: every decision you face is part of your preparation for the ministry. That includes seemingly simple matters like—

- Doing a take-home test
- Filling out income tax papers
- Answering the question "Why were you late?"

- Finding a $20 bill on the floor
- Breaking a rule when nobody will know
- Hearing people say hurtful things about someone absent
- Seeing someone who is sitting alone and is obviously lonely
- Deciding whom to sit with for lunch
- Deciding whether to get up in the morning when you've promised to be somewhere
- Realizing that your friend has not told the truth
- Seeing that your relationship with someone is getting out of bounds

These and a thousand other decisions are both born from and give birth to our character. Ministers need a strong character or their ministry will probably collapse after a while. While God will help us develop character, He does not do it without our cooperation. God will provide opportunities for us to make decisions, and He will provide the strength to decide correctly, but we must make the actual decision. When we do, and continue doing the right thing, we develop character. Without it, our ministry will crumble. With it, we will become a model of what we want others to be.

education

Most denominations have a list of educational requirements that ministers must meet before being ordained. Usually, certain academic degrees or the completion of specific courses is required. Before you can be ordained, most denominations require that you finish four years at college. Some require that you complete three additional years at a seminary, a specialized training school for ministers that is similar to a medical school or a law school. Other denominations require only a college degree but stipulate certain courses that must be completed. Some denominations require the study of biblical languages like Greek or Hebrew; others do not. Some denominations give ordination exams, where candidates for ordination must take a battery of tests to demonstrate that they have an adequate understanding of the Bible, theology, church history, and practical ministry before they are ordained. Other denominations conduct in-person interviews to see what the prospective ministers know and what they think. A few independent congregations ordain their own ministers and have hardly any educational requirements (a few will even ordain men or women for the ministry right out of high school). Most denominations, however, have educational requirements for ordination.

> the ministry is a profession which has a knowledge base that you will need in order to "operate" spiritually on the souls of people

You will need to discover what level of education your own denomination requires and make sure that you get the training you need. Whatever the denomination's requirements may be, it's certain that you will need some learning to become a minister. You wouldn't think of letting a surgeon operate on you who was gifted at cutting but had never been to school, would you? You value your body too much to let just anyone fool around with it, even if they did feel strongly that they could help you. How much more important than the human body are the souls of men and women? Just being a wonderful Christian will not make you an effective minister. The ministry is a profession which has a knowledge base that you will need in order to "operate" spiritually on the souls of people. Ignorance is dangerous, and the outcome of ministry malpractice could be something worse than physical death—spiritual death for all eternity.

required training

So what sort of education do you need? Here's a list of areas in which you'll need to receive training.

Bible. As a minister, you will have to preach and teach the Bible, so you'll need lots of Bible courses along with *hermeneutics*, the science of explaining and interpreting the Bible.

Theology. As a minister, you must explain who God is, what He is like, and what the church believes about God, human beings, sin, salvation, the Trinity, the future, and how to avoid wrong beliefs that could harm the people. You will need courses in *systematic theology*.

Church History. As a minister, you will need to know where the church has been, how God has dealt with His people for the past two thousand years, and the difference between the Eastern Orthodox, Roman Catholic, and Protestant churches. You'll need to know about Lutherans, Presbyterians, Methodists, and Baptists and how your own denomination fits into the larger scheme of things. You'll need courses in *church history*.

Christian Education. As a minister, you'll be leading discipleship groups, Sunday school classes, small group ministries, and children's and youth programs, so you'll need to know how each age group learns and changes, and how to minister to its particular spiritual needs. To do that, you'll need courses in *Christian education* and *youth ministry*.

Evangelism and Missions. As a minister, you will be responsible to rally your people to win the lost, reaching across the street and around the world to carry out the Great Commission. You will certainly need some courses is *evangelism* and *missions*.

Worship. As a minister, you will constantly be called upon to lead your people in worshipping God, so you'll certainly need some courses in *worship*.

Church Rituals. As a minister, you'll officiate at certain rites and ceremonies of the church such as baptism, the Lord's Supper, weddings, funerals, and child dedications, so you'll want training in how to lead *church rituals*.

Preaching. As a minister, you are ordained to preach the gospel. Ministers must be more than activities directors, like they have on cruise ships (this includes youth ministers too). Your calling is to preach, so you'll certainly have to have some courses in preaching often called *homiletics*.

Leadership. As a minister, you will lead others. When the church ordains you, it will give you authority to both preach and lead. Leading church people is not as easy as one might think—so a course or two in *church leadership* will help.

Counseling. As a minister, people will come to you with personal problems: family problems, marriage problems, difficulty in raising their children, and a dozen other crises, so you'll need at least some courses in *pastoral care* and *counseling*.

Liberal Arts. In addition to being trained for ministry-specific tasks, a minister needs to be generally well educated. Ministers are professionals and often preach to people with college or advanced degrees. People do not want to listen to a minister who is ignorant of the general knowledge we expect of any educated person. So you will need courses in the *liberal arts* or *general education,* simply to become an educated person.

Specialized Training. Most degree programs allow room for you to specialize your training by taking *elective courses* beyond those that are required for ordination. For instance, you might take all of the above courses yet want extra training in youth work because you want to especially minister to teens. Or, you might want to specialize in music because you have a strong interest in worship leadership in addition to the general tasks of ministry tasks.

> people do not want to listen to a minister who is ignorant of the general knowledge we expect of any educated person

Character development is central to your preparation, but your education will supply you with the base of essential knowledge required for your profession. Most denominations require courses in the above areas. Some require more training than others, but most ministerial education programs have core requirements that are very similar to those listed here. You should find out what your own denomination requires by visiting its web site or consulting with your ordination committee or board.

education and passion

Don't fall for the idea that you can become a minister without developing a strong base of knowledge in religion. Can you imagine going to a dentist that never heard of a root canal? Would you trust such a dentist? You'd probably think he was a quack! When you enter the ministry, you won't want to have a blank look on your face when you hear the terms: *Eucharist, Neoorthodoxy, Gnositicism,* or *exegesis.* Many laypeople know these terms, so can you imagine being a minister and not knowing them? A well educated minister understands the thoughts behind the terms also. He or she understands who God is and what He wants, and is able to rally the people to do God's will on earth as it is done in heaven. To do this takes more than the passion of the heart; it takes a highly educated mind as well. Having passion without education is like running in the dark. Think again of a surgeon who is untrained and inexperienced but feels passionate about cutting people and doing operations. Passion is good, but passion without education can do more harm than good. The first rule in the medical profession might be a good one for the church as well—"First, do no harm."

On the other hand, you'll need to make sure that your education does not wring out your passion. It can do that, you know. This is an occupational hazard for ministers. We deal with the sacred so much that we can come to see holy things as ordinary. Constantly dealing with the holy can deaden the soul. There is a danger that we may lose our delight, our childlike enthusiasm, awe, and wonder about the things of God. Thus, while studying these sacred subjects, we must constantly remind ourselves of their lofty meanings. But even that is training for the ministry, because for the rest of our life we'll be dealing with sacred things and be tempted in exactly the same way. So while you get your education, let your learning enhance, focus, and enlighten the passion you now have. And the best way to keep your passion is to stay involved in a local church every single week while you are being educated for the ministry.

practical training

The third leg of ministerial preparation is practical training. Character develops your heart. Education develops your mind so that you have the knowledge base from which to minister. Practical training develops your hands, strengthens you for the actual doing of the ministry.

Think again of a dentist. What good is a dentist who has character and fantastic educational credentials but has never actually filled a tooth? Would you like to be his first patient? The ministry requires character and education, but it also requires practical preparation. It is important to be educated on how to minister to a person dying of cancer, but you need also to be trained in *actually doing it*. There are some skills your school can help you develop in the classroom, like homiletics (preaching). But your school can't wheel a dying cancer patient into the classroom for you to practice on as they die! You'll have to get much of your practical training in a local church. This is where people hurt, need help, get miffed, want to be converted, ask questions about doctrine, and so forth. The local church is where you will get the experience base to add to your character base and knowledge base.

Most ministerial education programs actually require a person to get local church experience. That training may be called a *practicum* or an *internship*. That's where you'll be assigned to work in a local church and learn the ministerial equivalent of drilling and filling teeth. You will actually get to participate in a real funeral, where you can test experientially what you learned in classes. In your practicum or internship you will try your hand at real-life ministry. You'll work under supervision so you can learn the ropes from a professional.

But you should not confine your practical training to these required experiences. You will want to get wide experience, even while you are still getting your education. If you are in a college or seminary program, your studies may demand first priority of your time, but you will not want to ignore the golden opportunity to gain practical experience *along with* your study. Some ministers say it is good to get practical training in a variety of sizes of churches so you will be prepared for both large and smaller church ministry settings. After all, you never know what you'll be doing next. Most ministers would advise you to get practical training in various areas of church work. Four years of practical experience in youth ministry may help you get a youth pastor job, but it may limit your ability to function in other roles for which a church might wish to hire you.

> if God has called you to the ministry, then He has called you to take the time and effort to prepare for life in this vocation

the call to prepare

A call to the ministry is a call to prepare. If God has called you to the ministry, then He has called you to take the time and effort to prepare for life in this vocation. In fact, you will continue to prepare for the ministry long after you finish your educational requirements. Many ministers today admit that they really didn't gain all the basic practical training they needed until they reached their thirties. Even after that you will continue to get training. Your education won't end when you graduate from college or seminary. Increasingly, universities and seminaries are offering online programs or weeklong intensive courses that allow ministers to stay sharp in the profession of ministry. You'll need to find ways to keep learning so that you don't get stale. All professions change, and the ministry is no different. New developments will require new knowledge, so you'll be going back to school off and on through your whole life. And certainly, your character won't be a finished product at age twenty-five. You'll experience decades of further development. Preparation for the ministry is both an initial requirement and an ongoing process.

So, where are you now? How is your ministerial preparation coming? Central to your preparation is the development of your character, who you really are inside. As your character develops, you will need education so that you'll have the basic knowledge required to safely and effectively do the work to which you are called. And while you are learning that base of knowledge, you will need practical training in the actual skills of the ministry.

Why? Why do all this preparing? Because we are dealing with the souls of men and women, and that makes the ministry a vocation with eternal consequences. We should not enter the ministry as passionate amateurs. We should approach our profession as well trained—yet still passionate—professionals. We need all three: strong character, solid knowledge, and practical training.

exploring your call

to share

1. Since character development comes from making right decisions, often on little matters, share one or two decisions you faced recently, or may face in the next few days, that help to shape your character.
2. Tell about an something you used to struggle with that has become pretty much a habit of obedience for you.

to discuss

1. Imagine and describe three kinds of ministers, one with high character but low education and experience, one with high education but low character and experience, and one with high experience but low education and character. What are the dangers for each of these pastors in the ministry? How might they strengthen the areas in which they are weak?
2. Is there a required sequence in the development of character, education, and experience? Do they always develop simultaneously, as suggested in the chapter, or do they sometimes take turns, with one leaping ahead while the others catch up? Discuss this question with someone else.

to do

1. From your denomination's web site, print off the educational requirements for ordination in your denomination. Keep the list for future reference.
2. Make a triangular chart with the one aspect of preparation at each corner: character, education, and experience. List your one-year goals for each area so that you will have a plan to develop in all three areas over the next twelve months.

Does God call a person to youth ministry for life? Does God call people to go to specific places, like Mongolia? When you are working in a church and everything is going great then another church asks you to move there, how do you know if you should go or stay? Does God sometimes call people, then change His mind later and release them from their call? Can you be called to the ministry and then called out of the ministry to do something different, like start a restaurant?

the difference between God's call and God's leading

If you are headed into the ministry, understanding the difference between a *calling* and a *leading* is important to you. Even if you use the terms interchangeably, you ought to know that they represent two different ideas. What's the difference?

calling versus leading

My *calling* is an inner conviction from God, confirmed by the church, that I am commissioned to lifelong vocational service as an equipping minister for the people of God. A *leading* is God's guidance concerning the specific place where I will serve and what exactly I will do to fulfill my calling. A calling is lifelong and general; a leading is usually temporary and specific.

For instance, people sometimes say "I'm called to youth ministry." What they usually mean is "I'm called to lifetime ministry and right now God is *leading* me to do youth ministry." A pastor might say "God called me to come to this church" when she really means "God called me to lifelong ministry and *led* me to come to this church."

God's calling is lifelong. It shouldn't change through life.[1] My *calling* is what God's wants me to do with my life, everything else is *leading*. A youth minister who becomes senior pastor of a church in her forties would not be denying her call, just getting a fresh *leading* from God.

> a calling is lifelong and general; a leading is usually temporary and specific

It is usually best to emphasize that you are called to the ministry rather than to specify where God seems to be leading you to right now. When you do talk about the direction God is leading you, you might use statements like these:

- I'm called to the ministry, and God is leading me to work with youth.
- I'm called to the ministry and being led into worship ministry.
- I'm called to the ministry, and God is now leading me into overseas missions.
- I'm called to the ministry, and God is leading me to work with children.
- I'm called to the ministry and believe God's current leading is toward local church staff ministry.
- I'm called to the ministry, and God had clearly led me to come to this church and this city.

---

[1]This book does not deal with the "what ifs" associated with the midlife career change experienced by some ministers. Some say that a call to ministry may not be for life but only *pro tem*—for a time. These folk argue that it is normal and natural for ministers to give up the ministry and switch to another career partway through life. This book does not enter that debate, since it is written to prospective ministers and not to those already in the ministry. To new ministers, we emphasize that there is near-unanimous agreement that ordination vows, like marriage vows, should not be taken without the intention to enter the ministry for a lifetime. Ordination vows are not always kept just as marriages sometimes collapse. But a prospective minister should consider ordination a lifetime commitment.

The call and ordination are from God; they are lifelong and unchanging. A leading of God is usually temporary and may change several times throughout your life. It is OK to say "I'm called to youth ministry," but when you say it you should recognize you are really not speaking of your *lifelong call* but of a *temporary leading.* To get a feel for how these two terms relate, consider this case study that shows how the two might intertwine throughout a minister's life.

case study: jason and jessica

Jason went with his youth group to a gigantic youth convention right after Christmas during his junior year of high school. At the convention, a speaker preached about the call to the ministry in one of the main sessions. He gave the example of Isaiah's call from Isaiah 6, then reminded the students that the call seldom is so dramatic, but can be just as certain, like falling in love. "You can know for sure that God is calling you into the ministry just as certain as you can know for sure you are in love," he said. Jason had had thoughts about making the ministry his life's career since he was a child, but he had gotten serious about it only recently, after his current youth pastor, Mike, had come to the church. Mike had mentored Jason by making him a sort of assistant to the youth pastor at the beginning of the school year. Mike had even said, "You'd make a great youth pastor, if God ever calls you to it."

Jason had been pondering the idea of youth ministry. But he concluded, "I would never want to be a regular pastor, doing funerals and stuff." At the end of the service, the convention speaker said, "If you have been sensing a call from God to the ministry, I invite you to come forward to say so."

Immediately Jason wanted to go forward. He didn't hear a voice or anything; he just felt certain in his heart that he should do something like this with his life. Jason stepped into the aisle and went to stand on the stage with scores of other young people. After the closing prayer, Mike was the first to seek out Jason. "Congratulations! I've been thinking that God had you in mind for the ministry."

> you can know for sure that God is calling you into the ministry just as certain as you can know for sure you are in love

Two years later Jason was a freshman, enrolled in a ministerial program at a Christian college while working as a volunteer counselor in a nearby youth ministry. When Jason became a junior in college he got a part-time job, fifteen hours a week, as a student youth director in a church of about one hundred people. Here were about a dozen teens. When he graduated from college, the youth group averaged more than twenty teens each Wednesday evening.

Upon college graduation Jason married Jessica and took a job in Iowa at a church of about two hundred, which had a youth group of about thirty kids. Two years later Jason was ordained, and his youth group now averaged more than fifty kids.

As time passed, Jason sensed the need for more education. Besides, Jessica, who had majored in music in college, now felt called to the ministry and wanted ministerial training too. In the summer Jessica and Jason moved to Kentucky to begin several years of seminary training. While in seminary, Jason was especially attracted to the work of discipleship and mentoring. He had been disappointed with the long-term effect of his youth ministry over the last six years. Many of the most active teenagers had graduated from their religion at the same time they graduated from high school. He was convinced that a deeper discipleship foundation had to be laid under teen's lives in order for ministry to have any lasting effect. He often heard in seminary classes, "The test of a youth ministry is not this week's attendance, but how many are attending church ten years later."

Jason's interest in discipleship nudged him into courses related to mentoring, discipleship, and Christian education. He began to develop a fervor for discipleship as he once had for youth ministry in general. He still had a passion to work with teens, but his real desire was discipleship, not general youth ministry or even youth evangelism.

In the spring of their senior year at seminary, Jason and Jessica developed their résumés together. They hoped to work together on the staff of a church. During mid-March, a senior pastor from Michigan visited the campus to interview students, and Jason and Jessica showed up for an interview together. Everything just seemed to click. They immediately sensed that their mission fit with this pastor's vision and values. And there were two jobs open at the church! One position was Minister of Worship, Jessica's specialty, and the other one Minister of Networking and Discipleship, which was Jason's dream job. After an April visit to the church and interview with the board, they were both hired, and they moved to Michigan.

Jason and Jessica loved the church and their work in Michigan. They both worked hard and, the discipleship and worship ministries at the church blossomed. While in Michigan Jason and Jessica had all three of their children, two boys and a girl. They wanted to stay in this church the rest of their life; the people were great, and the church was exciting.

But that was not to be. When Jason was thirty-six years old, his senior pastor was elected to become the Michigan district superintendent for his denomination. That left Jason and Jessica in limbo. Would the new pastor want them to stay, or would he want someone else? Several of the board members suggested that Jason consider being the senior pastor, but he said, "I don't think so. I'm really a better staff pastor." Time passed, and a search committee was named to seek a new senior pastor. The church leaders guaranteed Jason and Jessica that they would be retained for another year regardless of who was hired as senior pastor. But the committee could not seem to find a new senior pastor everyone could agree on.

Finally, in August, three board members showed up at Jason's home one evening. "We represent the whole board, which has decided to ask you to be our interim pastor for this next year while we continue the search for a new senior pastor." Jason was not sure what to do. He really liked working for another pastor and not being the lead decision maker, but he promised to pray about it.

In prayer Jason felt compelled by God to say yes. Not because *he* wanted to be the interim pastor but because it seemed like *God* was asking him to do it. So he agreed and filled both the discipleship and networking and senior pastor positions that year, supervising himself as one of the staff members (and supervising his wife, Jessica, too). Jason preached more that year than he was used to preaching, though Jessica shared half the preaching load. Jason also took on other duties of a senior pastor that were strange to him at first, but he did his best. The church responded, and in fact grew both spiritually and numerically for the next eight months.

> jason also took on other duties of a senior pastor that were strange to him at first, but he did his best

It was April fifteenth. Jason would remember that date because his taxes were not done when they came to the church that day. Gathered in Jason's office was the entire search committee, though his appointment book had only listed the chair of the search committee. They came into his office and announced, "We are here because we are unanimous in believing that you are the pastor God wants for our church, and we want you to pray about being the permanent senior pastor here." It almost took Jason's breath away. He was surprised and shocked. He had been looking forward to getting a new pastor so he could return to his full-time work in networking and discipleship. But he agreed to pray about it again.

> the church became known in that town as a collection of solid Christians

It took more than one day of prayer. It was two weeks before Jason felt peace about it. Finally, he sensed in his heart (and Jessica confirmed it) that this indeed was what God wanted him to do next. Jason became the senior pastor three weeks later, after a unanimous vote by the congregation. A unanimous vote had never been taken in that church before.

Jason built that church for the next eleven years and attracted a staff of other ministers who loved working for him. Jessica continued to be the church's worship minister, though when the work became too much to manage, the church hired a second worship staff person to help out. New people found Christ, and the church became known in that town as a collection of solid Christians of good character. Jason's ministry as senior pastor seemed to have two marks: a youth orientation (the teens always sat in the first four rows and loved his preaching) and a focus on discipleship, both emphases having been developed in Jason's early years of ministry.

Jason had felt that he was in over his head when he became senior pastor, so he enrolled in a part-time program to work toward a doctor of ministry degree at the same Kentucky seminary he had attended years earlier. It took Jason several years to complete the degree, working one or two mornings a week and spending several weeks each year in residency on campus. He never planned to become a college professor or anything, but he thought, "I've got fourteen attorneys, nine doctors, three principals, a school superintendent, and six college professors in my congregation. I need as much training as I can get."

Jason was forty-seven years old when the head of the ministry department at a Christian college in a neighboring state asked if he would consider joining the faculty to train future ministers. "You are the perfect candidate to teach our practical courses: you have youth experience, discipleship experience, and you've been a senior pastor." Jason was flattered by the invitation. He loved his church and had come to love preaching. His congregation had grown to more than a thousand people, and they often said his teaching style of preaching was exactly what they needed to help them grow spiritually. Jason prayed about the prospect of joining the college faculty. Jessica asked, "Can you make the switch from preaching to more than a thousand people of all ages to teaching thirty twenty-year-olds?" Jason thought he could, but continued to pray, but he just couldn't get clear guidance on this issue.

The opportunity put Jason in such a tailspin that he could hardly concentrate on his ministry. Finally, in frustration, he picked up the telephone and called Mike, the youth pastor he'd had in high school. Mike was now senior pastor of a medium-sized church at the other end of Michigan. "Can I drive over and spend the afternoon with you in prayer?"

"You bet!" responded Mike.

During a long afternoon of prayer and coffee with Mike, Jason found peace about his decision. He found peace in the same way he found it concerning every major decision to

> God's *calling* is lifetime and general; His *leading* shifts as He guides us through life

date: he came to an inner certainty that this is what God wanted—or at least permitted. Relieved, Jason hugged Mike and said, "You'll never know how much you've meant to me all these years." He hopped into his car with a smile returning to his face. After punching the speed dial button on his cell phone, Jason greeted Jessica's hello with, "It's clear now. God came through again, like He always does. I know the answer."

one call, many leadings

Jason and Jessica's story illustrates the difference between God's *calling* and His *leading*. Jason was called into the ministry at a youth convention. Everything after that was a leading. It was a leading that drew him to Iowa to do youth work. Based on a fresh leading from God, he later went to seminary and took the staff job in Michigan. When he was asked to be interim pastor, then senior pastor, it was God's leading that Jason sought. And it was God's leading that gave him certainty about whether to accept the job training ministers at a college. Likewise, Jessica had one call to the ministry, which came to her as she directed worship as a layperson. In fact, the story of Jessica's call and leading would be quite different if we were telling it alone.

God's call is a lifetime commission to the ministry. God's leading is guidance as to where and how we will work with His people. God's *calling* is lifetime and general; His *leading* shifts as He guides us through life. There is one call but many leadings.

exploring your call

to share

1. Tell about a leading you received from God that was under the umbrella of your calling, something you prayed about and sensed God's guidance about but was not your calling.
2. A leading sometimes comes along with a calling so that the two may seem to be the same thing. Tell about your own call and how you understand that to be different from where God is leading you right now.

to discuss

1. Do you think Jason accepted the job training ministers at the college or stayed where he was, as senior pastor of the church? If Jason and Jessica had listed the pros and cons of both options, what factors would they probably have listed for each job?
2. The author of this book believes, as do most denominations, that the call to the ministry and ordination are both given for a lifetime and are not temporary. Some people disagree. Discuss this idea. What do you think of it biblically, theologically, and historically.

to do

1. Draw a life map for Jason and Jessica's life together, representing all the forks in the road where they sought God's leading. Imagine them taking the other fork at some point and diagram those alternative futures on your map. Discuss what you discovered with someone else.
2. Interview a minister and draw a life map that represents his or her ministerial career. Show all the forks in the road and decisions faced. Collect from this minister at least five bits of advice about how to sense God's leading, and share that advice with someone else.

How will my call to the ministry affect dating and marriage? Does it limit my choice of who I can "get serious" with? Can I date or marry anyone I'm attracted to and work out career details later? Can I be single in the ministry just as easily as being married? What if I marry a person who is open to my calling but he or she has a change of heart after we're married? What happens when both of us are called, one to African missions and the other to inner-city ministry? How would we choose between the two? Does my marriage trump my call to the ministry? Which is the most important factor in making decisions about my future?

dating, marriage, and the ministry lifestyle

if you plan to be a married minister, this chapter is very important for you. Why? Go ask a few older ministers for their advice on being a married minister. Get their wisdom on this subject. You'll find that they will all say something like this: "Your marriage will influence your ministry. It will either double your effectiveness—or cut it in half." This chapter is offered in the hope of doubling your effectiveness by helping you understand the ministry lifestyle and what that means about whom you should date or marry. It won't be as helpful as talking to older pastors, but reading this chapter will get you thinking about the subject until you have the chance to interview an expereinced minister.

marriage

Your call to the ministry stipulates the sort of life you will live. While there are always exceptions, the lifestyle of most ministers has much in common with those who have taken this path before. Here are several aspects of the ministerial lifestyle that have a direct bearing on marriage.

ministers move around

While some ministers get to stay in one city for a decade or longer, most ministers move eight to ten times during their life's ministry, and sometimes more often. A minister shares this characteristic with a military officer: both move frequently as they are "stationed" for the sake of their service, not because of personal preference. Ministers move. It is the rare minister who spends his or her entire career in one church.

the lifestyle of most ministers has much in common with those who have taken this path before

Some people can't live such a migratory lifestyle. They want to get married and "settle down" for the rest of their life, perhaps even in their home state or near their relatives. Also, some potential spouses have nonportable careers. They may plan to own a business, for example, and wouldn't be able to move easily. While it is possible to run a local business and be married to a minister, the spouse in this case should know that living in one town is most likely a temporary arrangement.

In a sense, all ministers are *itinerant.* They move around. Usually, people who want to stay in one place for their entire lives do not marry ministers. And ministers don't marry them.

ministers are public figures

Ministers and their families live in the public eye. A minister's family life is not a totally private matter. Ministers share this characteristic with politicians, entertainers, and celebrities. People are interested in the personal and family lives of public figures. A minister can't say, "I work here, but when I go home that's my own life, and we can do whatever we please." A minister's spouse can't say, "I don't want to attend this church because I don't like the worship style. I'm going to the church across town instead." Well a spouse *could* say that, but there would be a price to pay.

Some people can't put up with living in the spotlight. It's not that people peek in the minister's windows all the time or that ministers have no privacy at all, but some people want complete privacy for themselves and their families. Those people will seldom marry a minister.

ministers work long hours

A minister has wonderfully fulfilling work, but it is not done in a forty-hour week. Most ministers work fifty to fifty-five hours a week (some work more), and they are usually on call the rest of the time. A minister shares this characteristic with professionals like physicians and business executives. A minister's work is never done. There is no time clock for a minister, so a minister never really "punches out" and leaves work behind. Most ministers are on call twenty-four hours a day. If a daughter of someone in your church has a serious auto accident and is rushed to the hospital, they'll call you, and you will immediately go to the hospital. If a key member of your church passes away while you are on vacation, guess what? You'll probably cut your vacation short to perform the funeral. In a larger church, the ministerial staff might work a rotation, passing around a beeper and taking turns doing emergency calls. But even then there are some things you would just have to do. A minister, like a doctor, is on call much of the time, even after working about fifty hours a week.

Your potential spouse might not be able to handle that schedule. He or she might imagine that married life involves spending every evening together, going out to dinner or watching television. Most ministers have two evenings a week with their families, but they spend the other four or five evenings a week in church work. After all, that's when

> most ministers work fifty to fifty-five hours a week (some work more), and they are usually on call the rest of the time

laypeople are off work and available for meetings, counseling, church services, youth meetings, and other activities. The spouse of a minister has to share his or her mate during the evenings. This does not mean that ministers are automatically poor mothers or fathers, it just means they have to work harder to protect the family time in their schedules.

People who expect their spouses to work only forty hours a week and be home every evening usually do not marry ministers. Ministers usually don't marry them either.

ministers sometimes live in parsonages

Since ministers move from time to time, some churches own a house for their minister to use so the minister doesn't have to keep buying and selling houses all the time. A church-owned clergy home is usually called a *parsonage* or *manse*. This arrangement is similar to that offered to military personnel, who often live in "base housing." Churches often build large parsonages, since they can't foresee how many kids their future pastors might have. Thus, a pastor living in a parsonage might actually have a larger home than he or she could afford if the church provided a *housing allowance* (added salary to be used for housing expenses) instead of a parsonage. Some churches, however, have very old or poorly maintained parsonages, so a minister might wind up living in a home that is far below the economic standard of his or her parishioners.

> ministers marry people who love the church and the ministry just as much as they do

The trend among churches is to provide a housing allowance and let ministers rent or purchase their own homes. The majority of churches, however, particularly those of average size or in rural settings, still provide a parsonage. Some potential spouses insist on having their own homes. They say, "I could never live in somebody else's house." Or they have high standards for the type of home in which they intend to live. The lifestyle of a minister would be hard for such people. People who are very particular about the home in which they live usually do not marry ministers.

who marries ministers

Apart from these relatively few issues, the lifestyle of a minister is overwhelmingly positive for marriage and child rearing, so there are plenty of "candidates" for a minister to marry. Who do ministers marry? They marry people who love them and love other people. They marry those who like to be with people and like to help people. They often marry people who love the church and the ministry just as much as they do, and sometimes they marry other ministers so they can serve together at the same church. Most of all, ministers marry people who are adaptable and flexible, people who can roll with the punches and adjust to new situations. Rigid, inflexible people seldom marry ministers. And, ministers seldom marry them.

dating

So can a person who is called into the ministry date anyone he or she chooses? Sure, but most ministers would warn you against getting serious with someone whose temperament is totally incompatible with the ministry lifestyle. But how would you know that without spending time together? Spending time together, hanging out, being "just friends," and dating can help you find out what sort of nonnegotiable issues the other person has about lifestyle. If you discover that someone you are interested in is incompatible with the ministry lifestyle, you'll want to let that relationship cool.

Then again, people change. Older professors and ministers chuckle when they hear twenty-year-olds ticking off a long list of nonnegotiables—things they insist upon in their future spouse. Older folk know that you seldom get your whole wish list. Most people will fall in love, and, with their heads swimming, think they've found "everything they ever wanted" in a mate. Love is blind— or least has a serious visual impairment. When people are in love they tend to see whatever they're looking for. Love exagger-

> **if the minister's spouse isn't on board with a ministry lifestyle, it creates extraordinary stress for the family**

ates. But then, twenty-year-olds don't always know who they are going to be or what they will value when they are thirty. The opinions they held very strongly at twenty may have evaporated, and they may hold exactly opposite views on some issues.

What does all this mean for dating and marriage? It means that a twenty-year-old who has always wanted to live their life in northern California, have a private life, marry someone who works a forty-hour week and has every evening off might change his or her mind at age twenty-one after falling head-over-heels in love with someone who is entering the ministry.

This is not to say lifestyle matters can be dismissed casually. There are few negotiables in the ministry life. It is difficult for a minister to be a broker between spouse and church, like the rope in a tug of war. Every minister feels some of that pressure already. If the minister's spouse isn't on board with a ministry lifestyle, it creates extraordinary stress for the family. So, while people do change, it's essential to discuss these issues with anyone that you consider marrying. If you have a relationship that's getting serious, you ought to have some chats about the ministry lifestyle. A man or woman who marries a minister marries the ministry too. It's a little bit like being the President's spouse. The spouse of the President is married to both the person and the job and becomes a public figure to the nation. A person interested in marrying a minister needs to give serious thought to the cost. No person should undertake a building project without first "counting the cost," determining what will be required for finishing the project. If you are getting serious with someone and have not had this chat, start by giving your boyfriend or girlfriend this chapter to read; it could guide your discussion.

The life of a minister's family can be extraordinarily meaningful and positive. Minister's homes produce dozens of times more future ministers than lay homes. Being married to the ministry is a great way to spend your life. But if a prospective spouse cannot accept the ministry lifestyle, then the relationship should be allowed to die, even if you are in love. Once you are married, your spouse could force you to leave the ministry. Before you marry, you still have a choice.

marriage and calling

choose carefully a person with the gifts and graces to serve at your side

So what happens if you get married and become ordained, then one day your spouse announces, "I'm finished. I refuse to be in a ministry situation any more. Either leave the ministry or I'm leaving you!" What will you do then?

While such situations are rare, they do happen. Many ministers can tell you such a story involving a fellow minister they met sometime. This is a tricky situation. Should you let your call trump your vow in marriage? Or is it better to leave the ministry in order to keep the marriage afloat? Which vow is preeminent?

Obviously, there are at two possible choices in that situation. If you ever face it, get plenty wise counsel, for neither choice is a pleasant one. This book was not written as a guide for people facing a ministry-versus-marriage ultimatum, but the issue is raised here to remind you that the selection of a spouse is a decision that has a significant impact on your ministry. A poor or uninformed decision about marriage could bring on this more painful choice later—a choice you hope to never face.

Choose carefully a person with the gifts and graces to serve at your side. If you can find a spouse who is also called to the ministry, so much the better! But even if you don't, at least find someone who loves God's church, loves people, and does not have rigid and inflexible notions about his or her future lifestyle. Then ask God to bless your marriage to each other. For marriage is a *means of grace*, an experience designed by God to make you both more holy. Also ask God to bless your marriage as a gift to the church, so that (even if you have no children of your own) your marriage will "be fruitful and multiply" among the spiritual children whom you serve.

singleness in the ministry

Because this chapter devotes a lot of time to questions of dating and marriage, you might get the idea that a single person can't be an effective minister. That is not true. Indeed, if you follow the logic of the Apostle Paul, a single person can be *more* effective as a minister. Single people are able to give undivided attention to church work. That is not to say that single people should work longer hours in the ministry than married folk (though they usually do). If you'd like to be married but just have not found a mate yet, who knows? In time you may find the perfect match. If you are single and never intend to marry, so much the better; you can more easily make Christ's church and His work your primary passion in life. A single person is not a half person. Indeed, if there are any half people around they are all married, for in marriage "two become one." Don't forget, though, that single people face unique challenges in the ministry. Review the chapter on women in the ministry to be alert to the difficulties a single male can face in getting a job.

Are you hoping to be a married minister? Seek a spouse, but seek wisely. Don't go overboard by creating such high standards that you never find a mate, and don't barter away your calling for a cup of love soup by settling for a mate who is incompatible with the ministry lifestyle. Your marriage can double or halve your ministry effectiveness. Choose wisely.

exploring your call

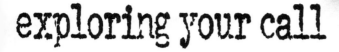

to share

1. Of the four characteristics of the ministry lifestyle
   that are mentioned in this chapter, which one do you think
   may be the hardest for you to accept as a prospective minister?
2. Tell about several characteristics or traditions of your home life that
   would be good characteristics for you to replicate in a minister's
   home.

to discuss

1. What are the advantages and disadvantages of a making a "shopping
   list" of characteristics that you want in a spouse? Are such lists helpful or not? Do you have one, written or unwritten? Tell about one
   thing on that list. Are the items on this list nonnegotiable?
2. What would you think about a situation where the spouse of a minister
   refused to stay married if his or her spouse wouldn't leave the ministry?
   What would you do, leave the ministry or let your spouse leave?
   Why? What Scriptures would guide your decision?

to do

1. Whatever you think of the shopping-list approach to evaluating a
   potential spouse, use this chapter and your own experience to make a
   list of the ten most important characteristics for the spouse of someone
   who is entering the ministry.
2. Interview an older minister and spouse who have raised a family in
   the ministry. Get their stories and advice on marriage and family
   matters in the ministry.

13

After I finish my education, how soon can I be ordained? Where will they hold my ordination service? Who actually does the ordaining? What if I get cold feet and want to back out? Will I need to do anything to prepare for my ordination service? Should I send out invitations? Can I pick the preacher? What will the service be like?

your ordination service

most denominations don't ordain people right after graduation from college or seminary. They expect ministers to get a few years' experience before being ordained for lifelong service. Ordination should not be taken lightly. Some prospective ministers, after getting some full-time ministry experience in a church, decide not to go through with ordination. That's OK. It's like an engaged person deciding, over time, that "this is not right for me." Most people would say "Whew—that was close" and congratulate you on not going forward with a marriage that you knew was not the best thing for you.

The same would be true if you decided not to be ordained. You might feel called, be confirmed by the church to begin preparation, graduate from college and seminary, begin to work full-time in a church and then realize that ordination is really not right for you. That is not a problem, other than that your education might seem to have been wasted. Like marriage, until you "tie the knot" in a public ceremony, you can still "get out of it." This is why most denominations require ministers to spend several years in actual ministry (some as long as a decade) before tying the knot in an ordination service.

> **ordination should not be taken lightly**

the wedding metaphor

The allusion to marriage is not accidental; an ordination service is very much like a wedding ceremony. It is a public ritual in which you make a life-long commitment. Can you ever "get a divorce" from the ministry? Yes, it sometimes happens, but you would never stand up to get either married or ordained with that possibility in mind. What Christian would get married thinking *If this doesn't work out, I can still get someone else*? None. Neither would anyone get ordained thinking *If this doesn't work, I can always become a lawyer.*

There are other parallels between ordination and marriage. Marriage begins with an *inner love* for a person, and ordination begins with an inner call. Marriage is *two-way* in that both the bride and the groom must agree to enter it, and the ministry is two-way in that both you and the church must agree (actually, God too, but He is represented by the church). Both marriage and ordination seek the *approval of others*. In each case, you will want to hear others say things like "I really see the two of you together for life" or "I can really see you being effective as a minister." People headed for marriage *spend time together*, getting to know each other. And if you are called to the ministry, you'll spend lots of time at church, getting to know God's work intimately. In a dating relationship sooner or later you might *make a decision* to get married. It's the same in the ministry. Eventually, you'll decide this is what you will do for your life. In marriage,

> **an ordination service is a public ritual in which you make a lifelong commitment**

the next thing you would do is to start *planning* the wedding. If you're called to the ministry, you will also plan for your ordination service. Finally there will be the *ceremony* of your wedding, or in the ministry, the ordination ceremony. And of course, both a wedding and ordination are supposed to lead to a *lifelong relationship.*

Ordination is not a new idea. The setting apart of spiritual leaders is an ancient custom in nearly all religions. In Christianity, the roots of ordination are traced to the Old Testament, where God's prophet was sent to anoint with oil first Saul and later David, making it clear that they had been chosen by God to lead the people. Even before that, priests had been set apart for special service to God. Each high priest was installed in an awe-inspiring ceremony.

In the New Testament, Jesus carried on the tradition of setting apart selected leaders by appointing twelve of His followers as apostles. The church at Antioch laid hands on Paul and Barnabas, commissioning them for service to the Gentile world. On their first missionary journey, Paul and Barnabas appointed elders in each church by laying on hands, a kind of precedent for what we do today in an ordination service. Throughout the early church, ministers were appointed and set apart for duty as elders or presidents of local congregations. For the two thousand years following the time of Christ there has been an unbroken line of ordination services as ministers and priests have taken their vows and been set apart for the lifelong vocation of the ministry.

you will want to prepare your heart for this most important worship service of your life

When a group of ministers gathers around you to lay hands on you and ordain you, you will know that these ministers one day had the hands of other, older minister laid upon them. And those ministers were set apart by a still older generation of ministers. Indeed, you might imagine a line of ordination services stretching back to the time of Christ. The ministry has been passed down from generation to generation through the laying on of hands—all the way to you. What a heritage!

preparing for your ordination service

Obviously, you will want to prepare your heart for this most important worship service of your life. If you have doubts about going through with it, it's better to call the whole thing off. This is not a trivial ceremony you can later dismiss. When you are ordained you may actually feel the power and anointing from God. In fact, people who took their ordination vows seriously and later abandoned the ministry often feel out of place, as if they have to make an excuse for why they are no longer in the ministry. Like a married person who no longer lives with his or her spouse, an ordained minister who leaves the active ministry often feels as if something is out of place. So if you are not called to lifelong ministry, don't get ordained. Instead, serve the church as a full-time lay worker. To be ordained is to make a serious vow. Prepare your heart carefully as you approach your ordination day.

But you will want to make other preparations as well. You'll want to invite the same people to your ordination service that you'd invite to your wedding. Invite people who know you; people who care for you. This is the high day in your life, so you'll want to send invitations to all your friends. And you might consider planning a reception or luncheon if your ordination council doesn't do that for you. It is a grand day, and you'll want to make it so.

elements of an ordination service

The order and style of your ordination service depends on your denomination's tradition. But most ordination services have a lot in common, for this rite is an ancient one. The service usually begins with an *invitation to worship,* and then there is worship through singing. Then a minister will offer an *invocation* of God's presence and assistance in the service. There will be a *message* delivered, almost always by a denominational representative who has many years of experience. You (and your spouse, if you are married) may be asked to sit on the front row, and the preacher will likely preach that sermon directly to you, with other people sort of listening in (again, very much like a wedding).

> the charge will say something about the lifelong and sacred nature of the call to the ministry and challenge you to take your ordination seriously

After the sermon, you may be *presented* to an important church representative who is presiding over the event. If others are being ordained at the same time, you will all be presented together. The presiding minister might then give an *acceptance,* announcing to everyone that you have been duly examined and found to be called and qualified for the ministry. There will usually be a

Scripture reading, generally one text each from the Old Testament, the Epistles, and the Gospels, following an ancient practice.

You will hear a public *charge* delivered to you, something like the challenge given at a wedding. This charge will say something about the lifelong and sacred nature of the call to the ministry and challenge you to take your ordination seriously. Then you'll probably face a public *examination*, where the denominational official or church representative will ask you publicly to answer a series of questions. This will be your opportunity publicly to confirm that you are called, affirm your belief in core Christian doctrines and the articles of faith of your denomination. You will also make a vow to preach the Word, live above reproach, and submit to the church's authority. These vows are not frivolous words used to fill up the service but are serious promises you must make. You should consider them beforehand and approach them at least as seriously as you

> those who ordain you will pray that some spiritual thing will happen to you at that moment—a filling, an empowerment, an equipping, an anointing—that enables you to minister supernaturally

would your wedding vows. Some denominations invite the spouse of the person ordained to make a *spouse's covenant*, since the ministry is a unique vocation and requires family support.

Finally, the bishop or presiding minister will lay hands on you—or perhaps have some or all the ministers present gather around and lay hands on you, performing the actual *act of ordination* and *prayer of enduement*. This prayer asks God to fill, empower, and gift you for the ministry. It is based on the Apostle Paul's reminder to Timothy that when elders laid their hands on him, something actually happened; it was not merely a ritual (1 Tim. 4:14). Those who ordain you will pray that some spiritual thing will happen to you at that moment—a filling, an empowerment, an equipping, an anointing—that enables you to minister supernaturally, not just from your own gifts and graces. For many, especially those who expect it in faith, something actually does happen. They become changed persons from that moment on. Some others feel no perceptible change at that moment. Either way, you should use that occasion to seek an enduement from God for a life of ministry, whether it comes at this moment or later on. For most ministers, the ordination service is the perfect moment to seek this supernatural power from God in faith.

Following the prayer, you may be presented with a gift, usually a Bible, as a reminder of the occasion. And those who have ordained you will extend *the right hand of fellowship,* which signifies that they have accepted you into the ordained ministry. After a *benediction*, there will likely be a *receiving line* where your friends will greet you and offer their congratulations and prayers for your ministry. There may also be a *reception* sponsored by the ordination council, or you might plan a dinner or reception on your own for your family and friends.

Ordination services vary quite bit, as you might expect, between denominations and regions of the country. But they generally include some form of the elements described here. Ordination is the solemn rite in which you are set apart for a lifetime of ministry. It is a high day of your ministry, and you'll want to have photos taken to remember it for the rest of your life. Some ministers commemorate the day by preaching a special sermon each year on the Sunday closest to that date. On the day you are ordained, you will join a line of priests and ministers that spans thousands of years of history, ministers who gave their life to lifelong service to God's people. It is a day for celebration!

exploring your call

to share

1. Tell about any ordination services you have attended.
   Describe what was similar to and what different from the
   elements described in this chapter.
2. Tell who you would certainly invite to your ordination, the people you
   would most want to be there and would be the most disappointed if
   they missed it.

to discuss

1. Talk about the parallels between a wedding ceremony and an ordination service, and extend those parallels through the rest of a ministry
   life. While there are always limits to such metaphors, what are the
   primary similarities that you want to keep in mind?
2. The more important the event, the greater the use of tradition. List the
   traditions in an ordination service that you think should be kept in the
   future and those you'd be willing to adapt or drop. How would you
   make an ordination service contemporary without losing value of the
   long tradition associated with this important ritual?

to do

1. Ask a minister to describe his or her own ordination service and tell
   both what made it meaningful and how it might have been done better.
2. Study the practice of laying on hands and anointing with oil in both
   the Old and New Testaments. Show your findings to someone else.

14

When you've finished school and been ordained, what's left? Is there more preparation, or are you now trained for life? What can you expect in the first decade of ministry? How will people treat a young minister? What should you look forward to in the first decade or so of local church ministry?

your first decade
of ministry

those of us who teach ministerial students see it often. Bright students leave college or seminary and enter the ministry, launching their life's work and assuming all preparation is in the past. Then they hit the wall. Things don't go as well as they had expected. Their great ideas are harder to implement than they had imagined. People don't flock to hear them speak at the church they've planted. Church people don't seem as impressed with them as their professors were.

Consider *Michael*. While only a junior in college, he launched a major community outreach program that reached more than three hundred high school students. Now Michael is pastor of a church that has hovered around thirty-two people for the two years he has been there.

Or, how about *Christine*. She delivered the senior address at a college chapel service and blew the socks off more than a thousand students. Last week the middle-aged ladies in the Women of the Word Bible study asked her to conduct one of their lessons. These women think they are giving this young girl a break by letting her teach a Bible study for a half dozen women. Or consider *Andy*. He always stood out in college and seminary. He was constantly told that he was the most promising ministerial student. Today Andy is in his third year of carving out a new church plant in a suburb of Denver, Colorado. About forty people attend—on a good week, that is.

> young ministers often find that the reality of being in the ministry is somewhat different than what they expected

What happens when a talented young person graduates from training and enters the ministry? In the first few years, many of them "hit the wall" as they come up against the hard realities of ministry. It is not as easy to plant a church as it is to lead a worship service on a college campus. Young ministers often find that the reality of being in the ministry is somewhat different than what they expected. Although they've been through several years of training in college or seminary, people begin to treat them as if they were freshmen again. When this happens, they sometimes come to doubt their abilities. They wonder if the problem is *this* church, a church that simply doesn't recognize their gifts and training, or whether they were perhaps mistaken when they believed God called them into the ministry. Some ministers actually give up and drop out in these early years, deciding they failed in the ministry or just weren't cut out for it.

extended preparation

You can do better than to give up when the ministry gets hard. Being prepared for these first years of ministry will help. You need to know what those first ten years might be like. This E-mail to *Michael*, a frustrated young minister, will help you get the idea.

Dear Michael:

Sure you feel like a failure. That's because you have your head screwed on wrong. You think now that you've entered the ministry things should just explode for you because you've prepared so well for the last four years. You imagine that life should be all downhill after graduation. That's the trouble. You're acting like you've finished preparing for the ministry. In fact, you've only just started. You're out of school, but not out of training.

Face it: you're still a student. So act like it! Keep learning. Keep growing. Keep developing. That's your job for the next ten years or so, learning to minister. For all practical purposes, you are still in school, but this time it is just the "college of life." You're a freshman again. If you see life from God's perspective, looking from the end of your life backwards instead of looking from this point forward, you'll recognize that you are in the second stage of what Leadership Emergence Theory calls *inner life growth.* You thought you were finished training

> you're acting like you've finished preparing for the ministry. you're out of school, but not out of training

when you left school, but you were just starting. College introduced the inner life growth stage. Now you are in the second half of that stage, the in-ministry half. Schooling got you started, but it represents only about 25 percent of all your training years.

When you look back on your life from age seventy, you'll probably categorize all of your twenties (and maybe much of the thirties) as preparation. From that perspective, which is also God's point of view, you will see this ten- to fifteen-year period as the time when God developed you into the servant He needed for your Big Task, which almost always comes later in life. You'll remember two parts to this preparation stage: the schooling years, and the early ministry years. You'll tend to see them both as training.

So, how will you respond to this idea of an extended preparation stage? The advice you would get from wise old ministers is to quit trying so hard to *succeed* and try harder to *develop*. Stop acting as if your whole ministry is going to be judged on what you do in your twenties. (That very thought will someday make you chuckle!) Realize that this decade or so of extended training is a common experience among leaders. Moses spent forty years in the desert; Paul spent a decade in Arabia and Cilicia before his emergence in Antioch; Jesus "wasted" ten years of adulthood in Nazareth. During this first decade of your ministry, worry less about success and more about growth. You're still in school. So let God develop your character, sharpen your skills, and deepen your spiritual life.

If you are in school now and preparing for the ministry you might sigh at the notion that there is still *more* training to get even after your education is finished. But don't be discouraged, God will use you in the lives of others while you are growing and learning. In most denominations you will have at least a few years after your education before you are ordained. During those years you will be getting more experience, making sure of your calling, and developing competence. In fact you will probably be ordained part way through the first decade of experience, sometimes as quick as a few years after your initial education is complete. But, even after you are ordained you'll have lots of development ahead of you. So, what are the "courses" in this decade-long period of your life? There are at least three: developing character, sharpening your skills, and deepening your content.

> let God develop your character, sharpen your skills, and deepen your spiritual life

character development

College and seminary do not prepare you completely for the storms you may face in your forties and later. Most young ministers are not even ready for success. Few things destroy a young leader faster than premature success. God needs more time to prepare you for your later work. Your character needs to be refined. Your heart needs to be worked on. At twenty-five, you may have experienced many temptations, but not enough *kinds* of temptation. Temptation is great preparation for future ministry. Facing and beating temptation develops the character God wants from you in the future. At twenty-five, you've not had enough criticism or opposition, and you've not experienced great failure. All of these are experiences that develop the strength you will need for the Big Task that lies ahead of you. During these years of extended preparation, let God refine your character. Give Him a decade or more to do it. That's your primary assignment in this phase of your life.

sharpening skills

When you graduate from college or seminary, you'll probably think you are pretty hot stuff. When you compare yourself to what you were as a freshman, your growth will seem impressive. But God has so much more in store for you. How will He develop your skills in speaking, leading, managing, and, most of all, working with people? He will develop them as you *use* them. You try. You fail. You evaluate. You adjust. You try again. You learn. You copy others. You ask questions. You read. You make mistakes. You pick up the pieces and try again.

You will want to find a place of service where you can "fail forward." You'll want a place where you can try new things, get correction from wise leaders, improve yourself, then try again. Look for a place where people will help you improve. Certainly you don't expect your college or seminary homiletics class to provide all the learning you'll need to become a great preacher. And those Christian education courses you took couldn't provide all the Bible teaching or group skills you'll need for the rest of your life. You are still in training for preaching, teaching, and leadership for at least a decade after you graduate. This will be a ten-year lab course in the actual

> you are still in training for preaching, teaching, and leadership for at least a decade after you graduate

skills of ministry. You'll learn. You'll read. You'll get evaluation. You'll improve. The first ten years of your active service in the church is really a decade-long residency.

deepening content

When God does finally give you your Big Task, what will you say? What will be the *content* of your message? A few years of upper level courses in Bible and theology can't provide all the wisdom you'll need to make your life's major impact. It takes years of experience to discover the deepest needs of human beings. It takes years of walking close to God and understanding His plan to really know His will for the church. It will take at least a decade to hammer out the implications of your own theology. You may know theology based on college and seminary studies, but when you hit the real-world local church, you will have to revisit everything you believe in order to develop practical applications for preaching and leading God's church.

How could you be an expert on marriage and raising children at age twenty-five? You could read and study and interview parents, but a decade of experience raising your own son or daughter will bring bonus wisdom and credibility you could never get otherwise.

How about Scripture? Most men and women entering the ministry, even after seminary training, have merely scratched the surface of God's Word. Nothing will drive you deep into the Scriptures like preaching to needy people. All these experiences develop *content* in your life. They give you something to say to people. They supply you with the wisdom that people hunger for. Of course, you will continue deepening your content throughout your life, but during these first ten years you will see a giant leap in the "finishing school" of life.

Sometimes graduates of seminary or college say to God, "Give me my Big Task now Lord, and I'll cram for it. I'll develop the character, skills, and content I need quickly." But be careful what you ask for. God may answer that prayer. You may find yourself leading a ministry far greater than your character, skills, and content. And you may fail too early in life, where the consequences are too big. Instead, wise ministers go for the long haul. They know God develops character, skills, and the content over many years and seldom accelerates the process. So even when you have finished your education, there is ahead of you a decade of greater development. Developing your character, skills, and content is like raising children. It takes years to get the job done, and it can seldom be hurried without serious consequences.

going the distance

Your first decade in the church is a period of extended preparation for ministry, but even that won't make you a finished product. People change. Ministry methods change. Society changes. Satan shifts his strategy constantly. Thus you will need to keep learning and growing throughout your life. This learning curve will seem steepest when you are young, but there will be other periods of your life when you will leap ahead in learning. Many ministers go back to school—even after many years in the ministry—to sharpen their minds and develop their skills. Ministers frequently attend worship services and seminars to enrich their spiritual lives and get new ideas. In answering the call to the ministry you are answering a call to lifelong learning.

As a young person, it will be tempting for you to cram a whole life's ministry into the first decade. Unfortunately, some actually do that! They are so passionate about ministry, so committed, so intense, that they burn out by the end of their first decade in the ministry, some even before that. They tried to win the world to Christ as if they were the only soldier in God's army. They take little time off, have no hobbies, skip their vacations, and do without sleep. And sure enough, their ministries explode with growth! They soon begin to get famous in their district or denomination. But six, or eight, or ten years later they are gone—*poof!*—like falling stars that disappear, burned out and cold. They did indeed cram their entire ministry into a few years, then leave the active ministry before age thirty-five. This is *burnout.*

> many ministers go back to school—even after many years in the ministry—to sharpen their minds and develop their skills

Some others *flameout.* They lose their heated passion and become spiritual zombies, finally abandoning their call. Still others *spin out*, getting involved in immorality that gets them removed from the ministry. Either way, if you burn the candle of life at both ends you can burn it up too fast.

To avoid burnout, flameout, or spin out, you (and you alone) must learn to pace yourself. Ministry is not a hundred-yard dash. It isn't even a marathon! Ministry is a long distance trek. It is like backpacking a thousand miles or more. It requires taking a long view, pacing yourself, and making sure you don't break your (spiritual) ankle and get eliminated from the journey. While there are times when a burst of speed is needed, a trek is completed with a dogged, determined, steady pace. God is more interested in your next fifty years of ministry than your next fifty weeks. Go for the long haul!

exploring your call

1. Talk about what you suspect you will still have to learn after you've finished school. Name some things that you feel inadequately prepared to do and others that you feel well-trained to undertake.
2. List other professions that have a decade or more of extended preparation. That is, professions in which the initial training doesn't produce a complete professional.

to discuss

1. List some strategies that ministers can use for coping with "hitting the wall" in their first ten years or so of ministry. What can we do to survive that experience?
2. If ministry is always changing and there are always new skills to acquire, how can a minister stay on the cutting edge and avoid becoming out of touch or ineffective?

to do

1. Interview an active minister and find out what his or her first decade of ministry was like. Where was it spent, what type of ministry did he or she do, what lessons were learned?
2. Make an Action Plan Reminder Card for yourself. List the dates that will likely include your first ten years of ministry beyond school, then list "Reminders to Me" that you can refer to during that decade. Preserve that wisdom for later.

epilogue

seeing your life through the rearview mirror

f you determine to go for the long haul in your ministry, it is very likely you'll come to the end of your life having served fifty (or even more) years in the ministry. Imagine yourself then, as an old man or woman, at perhaps seventy-eight years old. You will probably be retired by then, though you might still preach at nearby churches from time to time when a pastor is on vacation. You'll most likely be a very happy old person, and wise too. People will come to you sometimes to ask your opinion. Your neighbors in the retirement community where you live will call you Pastor or Reverend when they greet you on your morning walk. Younger folk in your church (middle-aged folk actually) will come to you for advice. They'll ask you to tell them about how it was "back at the turn of the century." They'll love hearing how you used to use a giant computer that weighed more than a pound and that you actually had to input information with your fingers.

Imagine for a moment that you and your lifelong spouse are sitting in the living room in the evening. The sun has just set, but your eyes have adjusted and you still haven't turned on any lights. It's a sweet time. You chat quietly about your life together, and especially your ministry. By then you will have served at seven or eight churches. Just as other people recall the cars they've owned, you'll recall churches—one by one. There will be laughter, chuckling, and an occasional tear in your eyes. Why? Because you'll mostly talk about *people*. The greatest joy (and the greatest trial) in your ministry will have been the people. You won't be talking much about the youth center you built in your thirties. And you'll not spend too much time recalling the booming numerical growth of that church you pastored in your forties. You won't even speak much about the gigantic worship center you led that congregation to build in 2042. You'll talk mostly about the *people* you helped along the way.

You'll remember *Carol*, that neighborhood girl who started attending your Sunday school at age eleven, became a Christian, and still writes to you every Christmas. Carol leads the choir and teaches children's church in Tucson now.

You'll remember *Chad*, the single guy who came to your second church only "because they had baseball." Chad felt called to the ministry, served his whole life in church work, and is now the pastor of the very church you attend as a retired person! You'll thank God for how He changed Chad.

You'll talk about *Angelina* and how she came to you in your first youth group, rebellious, angry, and dead set against God. And you'll retell the story, taking turns tossing in the details, of how God changed Angelina's life and how she decided to go to a Christian college even though nobody in her family had ever even graduated from high school. You'll have lost contact with Angelina by now, but you'll stop in the twilight quietness of your living room and pray for her, wherever she is.

You'll remember *Hank* and *Mary Anne* and how their marriage was on the rocks when they called you. "When was it dear? Oh yes, long after midnight." You'll retell the story of how you worked with them, prayed with them, counseled them, and how they decided to give it "one more try." You'll talk about how Hank became a solid and steady layman in that church and how Mary Anne took over the worship ministries for several years. What a joy to remember Hank and Mary Anne.

You'll wonder where *Jacob, Tim, Patty, Sue,* and *Sharon* are now. You'll tell stories about each, there in the quiet darkness—how God transformed their lives as you ministered with God in that church. There will be others whose names you can no longer remember. "What was the name of that guy that came to that Easter Techno-Pagent back in the 30s . . . the one who took us out to dinner?" Neither of you will be able to recall his name. But you'll remember his story, how he went back to Poland and led his whole family to the Lord, then did his ministerial training on what they called "the Internet" back then. You'll tell how he started those three churches in Poland, and you'll wonder how they're doing.

There will be others. Dozens more. No, *hundreds!* If you could only remember it well enough, you would recall thousands of people God had sent your way so that they could benefit from your ministry.

Your spouse will doze off as you tell one particularly long story. You'll glance that way and chuckle, but not stop. You'll quietly lower your voice and tell the end of the story anyway—to yourself. And to God. You'll start to doze off yourself and smile softly, then say, almost under your breath, "Thank you, Lord. Thank you Lord for calling us to the ministry—it's been a wonderful life."

Spending your life in the ministry is the single most fulfilling way to invest the years that God has given you. If He has given you the privilege of receiving a call to the ministry, by all means, take Him up on the offer! It is a wonderful way to spend your active years—and it makes a wonderful life to look back on at the end!

appendix

frequently asked questions about the call to the ministry

Q: After reading this book I've decided that I'm really not called at all. What should I do?

a: Seek God's direction for how you should invest your life. Don't feel bad that you investigated spending your life in the ministry. It is better to seriously consider it and discover that you are not called than to never seriously consider the ministry if you were called.

Q: I was ordained as a minister decades ago, but now I'm out of the active ministry due to health problems. Am I out of God's will?

a: Not at all! Find a way to meaningfully contribute to God's kingdom where you are, and move on. Your "early retirement" will provide lots of opportunities for ministry, just as if you were a retired minister.

Q: My denomination appoints pastors to churches without a vote of the congregation or the consent of the minister. I'm not sure I could submit to that system.

a: If you can't submit to the authority of your denomination, and God won't change your heart, then you'll have to find another denominational home.

Q: I'm more of a group-type leader. I want to help a group find out what God is calling it to do rather than being a Moses-type leader who goes up to the mountain and gets a vision from God then comes down to cast it before the people.

a: Great! We need more of your kind in the church.

Q: Are there any sort of special ethical things about the profession of the ministry that I should know about?

a: By all means. Whole books are written on the subject. The way to start learning more is to look up your own denomination's statement of ministerial ethics. It is probably posted on the denomination's web site.

Q: I've met several people who were taking courses so they could get ordained because they wanted to reduce their income taxes. Is that possible?

a: Yes, it is true that in the United States, tax laws give ministers a break. But reducing your income tax bill is the wrong reason to be ordained. It's not just wrong; it is outright shameful. Getting ordained to save taxes would be like getting married to save taxes. It is simply the wrong reason to do a right thing. However, you will probably meet ministers who do all kinds of things that are beneath their dignity. In every profession there are a few bottom-feeders who give the rest a bad name.

Q: Can the church nix the call of God? That is, if I know I am called, but my church won't ordain me, does that mean my call is rejected?

a: Only if you cannot find any church anywhere in the world that will recognize your calling and ordain you. A minister with no congregation to receive his or her ministry is like a tree falling in the woods with nobody around to hear it. If you are truly called, some denomination will recognize that call. Otherwise, you may have misunderstood God's voice.

Q: Who can they call a *pastor* in a church, just ordained people or any staff member?

a: A church can refer to anyone it wants to as a pastor, from the senior preacher to ordained staff people, to part-time lay staff, to Sunday school teachers. *Pastor* really means *shepherd*, so nearly anyone could hold that title if he or she is responsible for shepherding others.

Q: My denomination rejects the ordination of women, so that part of this book is totally useless to me. I strongly disagree with your position.

a: That's OK, your denomination will eventually see the light—and so will you, I hope.

Q: I think I want to become an itinerant speaker and travel around doing youth conferences and large events. My dream is to speak someday to thousands of people at large crusades in major cities.

a: Be faithful with little things, and God could make you famous some day. But be careful of dreaming too much of greatness as a speaker. That is a great snare for ministers. Instead, focus your vision more on the people who will hear you than on yourself as the speaker. Picture their changed lives instead of your own impressive preaching and fame. If this vision is from God, be faithful and it could happen. But don't wander away from the local church on your way there, for the local church is God's primary tool for bringing His kingdom to pass on earth.

Q: I would like to own a Starbucks and run it as a ministry. I can really get into that kind of ministry.

a: Starbucks makes great coffee, but a coffee shop does not a ministry make. Do your Starbucks thing, but don't pretend it is the ministry. Do your ministry working at your secular employment, just as every other Christian should do.

Q: **Hospitals and nursing homes make me sick. If I have to go into those places as a minister, I won't be able to take it.**

a: Either seek God's gifts of compassion, mercy, and love so you'll be able to do this, or find another life calling besides the ministry.

Q: **You say that a minister should have a strong desire to do ministry. I don't have that desire. I never did. And yet God has called me to the ministry.**

a: The desire may yet come, especially as your love for God and His people increases. Occasionally, God calls people who have no desire to serve Him, but this is rare. If He did this with you, He must have something mighty interesting in store for you. You may say "let this cup pass from me," but you'd better follow it with "nevertheless, thy will be done." Give it time.

Q: **I think I have been experiencing a testing of my call recently, but I don't know if it is from God (who is trying to test my commitment) or the Devil (who is trying to destroy my future as a minister). Can you help me decide?**

a: What does it matter? In either case, what you should do in response to the testing is the same, right?

Q: **I have had some serious sins in my past life, and I wonder if God is making a mistake by calling me into the ministry. How can I lead others when I did so many terrible things before I was a Christian?**

a: Welcome to the club! You are in it with people like Moses and the Apostle Paul.

Q: **I have never been a leader in my life, but I think God is calling me to the ministry. How can I be a minister when I can't lead?**

a: You can learn to lead just as you can learn how to play basketball.

Q: I am not sure if I should become an ordained minister or just serve as a layperson on the staff of a church. How can I decide?

a: When in doubt, take the ordination courses. You can always decide later that you don't want to be ordained, but if you bypass the ordination courses now and then decide that you do want to be ordained, you'll have to go back to school all over again to get the training. Taking the ordination courses doesn't mean you have to be ordained, but you can't get ordained without them.

Q: How has the appearance of so many megachurches changed the ministry?

a: It has blurred the line between ordained and lay staff ministry. Churches don't like to make distinctions between their staff members, so they tend to use titles like Pastor or Reverend for all full-time workers. And many churches have positions for ordained ministers who never preside over communion or preach. Some ordained ministers serve on the staff of a church and preach only every few years. Most denominations are expanding their concept of ordained ministry beyond what it was in the days when most every church had only one pastor.

Q: How does all this apply to missions and intercultural work?

a: In the same way. A missionary might be either an ordained minister or a layperson.

Q: I would like to found a parachurch organization where I could develop soccer teams that raises support then go around the world and play soccer as a witness for Christ.

a: OK, but make sure this is not an attempt to make your hobby into your calling. And be careful of becoming a "fund raising scheme" that drains relatives and the local church of money that ought to be used for other things. Also beware of the lack of accountability that sometimes ensnares those who found their own ministry organizations. Finally, serve a half dozen years in a local church before you begin your soccer ministry. After all, you have no right to be sent out by the church unless you are in it in the first place.

For the next five years, get involved in a church and start organizing soccer teams for the kids in the church. Then, after you have been faithful in these little ministries, you might start thinking about launching a big parachurch ministry. But see what the body of Christ says about it after you've given five years in local church ministry.

Q: I know a high school teacher who was filling in at an independent church, and they ordained him even though he never planned on being a full-time minister. He kept his job teaching, and when the church got a preacher he went back to being a layman. Is this kosher?

a: To that church it might be, but not to most denominations. Local churches sometimes do things frivolously and do not always understand what they are doing. It's the same with individuals. In the case you cite, the person probably experienced an "ordination of convenience," which meant no more than what was said at the time: "We want you to be our temporary pastor *pro tem*." You would have to talk to the teacher to find out if he really had been called to lifetime ordained ministry or was just filling in as a lay preacher for awhile. Remember, independent churches do not have a denomination to guide them in such matters, so if the majority of the people want to do something, they can simply do it. Well-run independent churches have careful bylaws or are connected to an informal association of similar churches so they're less likely to do something foolish. But there are a few lone ranger churches which do just about anything they please.

Q: I plan to work in children's ministry for the rest of my life. Should I go for ordination or be a lay staff worker?

a: It is up to you. Do you feel that God has called you to ordained ministry? Ask the ordination board of your denomination for guidance.

Q: I am about to graduate and should be ready to enter the ministry, but I feel more inadequate than I did when I was called as a high school senior.

a: You're not alone. You will always feel a certain inadequacy for the incredible responsibility of being a leader in God's church. And if you ever lose the feeling that you need to rely on God's strength, then you really will be in trouble.

Q: I was raised in one denomination, but I went to school at another denomination's college. Now I can't decide which denomination I should settle into.

a: Pray about this for a few weeks. Find five people who know you well and ask their advice. God often speaks through others. You might want to talk to leaders in both denominations and get their advice. Most people would give their home denomination the first chance.

Q: The guy I am dating says he could never be a "minister's wife," but I really love him, and I am certain I am called. What should I do?

a: Well, could he be a minister's *husband?* Seriously, you need to either get a new calling or a new boyfriend. You could wait for him to change, but don't get so entangled in the relationship that you abandon your calling. The central question is this: are you really called? Once you answer that question, the rest is simple.

Q: Do ministers really work fifty to fifty-five hours a week?

a: Most do, some more. And there are some slackers that work only a few hours a week even though they look busy the rest of the time. Although most ministers do work fifty to fifty-five hours a week, when ministers attend worship or Sunday school, that counts as work—which it is, for them. So the average layperson who works forty hours at a job and then gets highly involved at church might easily put in a combined fifty hours on both activities.

Q: How much does a minister get paid?

a: Ministers' salaries are all over the map, from the part-time pay of country pastors to the very comfortable compensation of senior pastors at multimillion-dollar suburban churches. Few ministers get rich off the ministry; we can say that for sure. But none starve either. Many part-time ministers also have full-time jobs doing other things, so their total income is not as bad as it might seem if you looked only at their church salary. A good rule of thumb some churches use to determine their pastors' pay is this: "We will pay our minister the average of the salaries of our church people who work full-time." Their idea is to have the minister fit in economically with the people of the church.

Q: **I saw an ordination service last summer when I was traveling with a singing group, and it was nothing as nice as you suggested in your book. It was kind of frivolous, actually. Why is that?**

a: As sometimes happens with other solemn rituals like weddings or communion services, those presiding at an ordination service don't always understand its importance. That's why some denominations require that an official of the denomination must preside over all ordination services. That helps to ensure that it is not depreciated. But people sometimes do sacred things frivolously. Some Christians have even taken the Lord's Supper lightly. I once observed a youth retreat where a youth pastor served communion by tossing croutons and grapes from the communion table to each member in the audience while the whole group cheered. When someone missed catching a grape and it fell to the floor, others would sometimes squish it underfoot and call for a fresh grape. Christ intended Holy Communion to be a sacred rite, but that's no guarantee that someone won't desecrate it while trying to be "relevant." Your denomination is the guardian of the sacred service of ordination, and their treatment of it may indicate their low or high view of the ministry itself. Of course, even some denominational leaders and boards lack the ability to make this service be what it ought to be. If you get stuck in such a situation, you might even offer suggestions yourself. If all else fails, get on that committee in the future and make a difference for future ministers!

Q: **You keep saying that the call and ordination are for life, but I heard somewhere that half of all ministers drop out of the ministry in the first ten years.**

a: And many marriages end in divorce too. The call and ordination should be for life, but people fall away. However, the statistics you heard probably counted all people in one of the ministry tracks, including those preparing for ministry. Many drop out before ordination, which is why most denominations delay ordination for a while: to give people a chance to change their minds before taking the ordination vows.